To Enrig

I want you to know
you are fully known and
loved by God.
"GTA"
Greater Things Ahead

The Set-Up:

A STORY OF DEFEAT
TURNED VICTORY

Your Friend,

[signature]

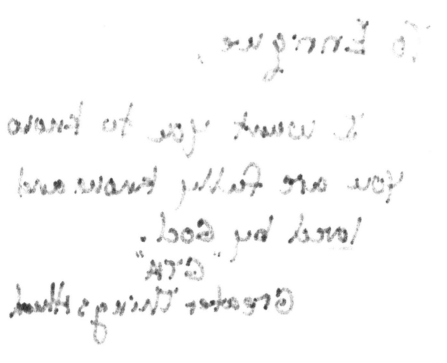

Xulon Press
2301 Lucien Way #415
Maitland, FL 32751
407.339.4217
www.xulonpress.com

© 2019 by Danny Williford

All Scripture references are from The Holy Bible, English Standard Version. ESV® Text Edition: 2016. Copyright © 2001 by Crossway Bibles, a publishing ministry of Good News Publishers.

Printed in the United States of America.

ISBN-13: 978-1-54567-651-6

The Set-Up:

A STORY OF DEFEAT TURNED VICTORY

DANNY WILLIFORD

XULON PRESS

The Set Up is a story of defeat turned victory. It is dedicated to everyone who is waiting for their biggest defeat to be transformed into their greatest victory.

Acknowledgements

To my family and friends: I'm so grateful for each of you. Thank you for your prayers, for never giving up on me, and for believing that the crazy man was not the real Danny.

To my wife, Kim: Thank you for your constant support and believing the promise that God gave to us! I could have never imagined the kind of relationship that we have. You are the ultimate set-up.

To my children, Trinity and Micah: When I see you, I'm reminded of the goodness of God. You are the biggest gift in my life. I'm very proud to be your Dad.

To my church, Freedom Fellowship: Over the past 16 years you've been part of my transformation. God knew exactly what my family needed when he placed us there. Thank you for your care and for walking beside us on this Journey. You are the definition of intimacy with God and intimacy with others.

Last but not least, to John Maxwell: You've impacted my life thru DVD's, books, conferences and JMT mentorship. I would not be where I am today if it wasn't for the leadership lesson's I've learned from you. Without a doubt God has "set you up" to add value and make a difference in the lives of people around the world.

Table of Contents

Introduction
"Set-Up"

"The Cross was a set-up. It wasn't set up by Judas,
it wasn't set up by Herod, it wasn't set up by the Sadducees.
It was set up by Heaven to fulfill the Scriptures.
Death didn't trap Jesus, Jesus trapped death...
Sometimes victory does not look like victory." [1]

-Pastor Steven Furtick

I know a thing or two about being set-up. In fact, there is very little about my life that would be the way it is right now were it not for set-up after set-up.

---

[1] Steven Furtick, "The Thirst Trap" (speech, Charolette, NC, April 02, 2017), Elevation Church, https://elevationchurch.org/sermons/the-thirst-trap/.

One of these set-ups had me surrounded, with police aiming weapons of war right at my face, screaming at me to "Get down! Get down! Get down!"

At the time, I believed that those who I ran with had my back, yet I was to later find out that I had been involved in an actual set-up.

Someone had snitched.

It was a moment that literally changed every fiber of my being, although in ways I was not at all aware of at the time.

Another set-up occurred in a dark, dingy prison cell with a crazy man yelling at me. I'll tell the rest of this story in the pages that follow, but suffice it to say that this was quite the experience.

If the first set-up changed every fiber of my being, the second one destroyed me. No, I don't mean that figuratively. This changed who I was so much that I never looked the same again. Nothing, and I mean nothing, from that point forward remotely resembled who I was before.

I can think of many more times that I was set up, be it by a snitch who I thought I could trust or by the police who I had such disdain for, but those are not the set-ups that changed me the most. What I have learned all of these years later is that my entire life has been one big set-up.

The word "set-up" can mean two different things, depending on the situation. In some cases, a set-up can cause an innocent man great harm by framing him for something he frankly had no involvement in. Now, I have made my fair share of mistakes. In fact, there is no more of an understatement than to say that I have made mistakes. I have screwed up more times than I can count. With that said, I have also been framed. People have taken advantage of my screw-ups and framed me for things

I didn't do. I've been set-up in this way more times than I can count.

A set-up, however, can also cause a guilty man to rightfully face justice. Remember the police cars, the sea of officers with looks of revenge on their faces yelling at me, an in-the-moment pathetic middle class kid looking down the barrels of a dozen of guns, to "Get down!"? That was no unfair set-up. Sure, it seemed unfair at the time, but I was guilty as charged. I had royally screwed up, and now, I was trapped. This kind of set-up, you see, can seem like it's the end of the road. That's how I felt. Laying down on that cold pavement, being roughed up by cops about to throw me into a prison cell for God knows how long, I thought this was the end of the road for me.

Boy, was I wrong.

When we are set up, not framed for something we didn't do but caught red-handed in our guilt, no matter how much it appears that we have reached the end of the line, in the most important ways, it is a glorious beginning.

Have you ever created a web of lies? I don't mean one little white lie to your wife about the dress she's about to go out in or to your boss about how sick you really are when you call in. I'm talking about lies that build, one on top of the other. As much as you try to not get caught, wanting to spin that web as big as possible, how good does it feel when you actually are caught? Sure, you feel terrible right when it happens, but not too long afterwards, you realize you have a chance. A chance to tear down the web and start fresh.

No more hiding. No more sneaking. No more lying awake at night figuring out your next move.

That's how I felt. Sure, not immediately, but eventually. The set-up I thought had ruined my life actually set me on a new course I had been designed to be on. I thought I had been set-up by a no-good snitch who couldn't keep his mouth shut for a second if it meant saving himself.

It turns out I was wrong.

Who set me up? It wasn't the snitch but rather the One who ended up talking to me in that dark, dingy prison cell the night everything about me changed. In that cell, I would recognize that the set-up was so different than what I thought it was.

Looking back on it now, all I can think about are the words of another prisoner from millenniums ago:

"And we know that for those who love God all things work together for good, for those who are called according to His purpose."[2]

Let me pause for a second before moving on. Perhaps you are as weary as I am when someone yanks out this verse. You can probably hear the voices of well-meaning but ignorant Christians in your past.

"Don't be upset! God will make this into a good thing!"

"Why are you sad? Don't you know that for God's people nothing is bad?"

"Well, you must not be right with God because if you were, He would have caused this situation to work for good."

I hate when people take this verse out of context. In fact, I hate it so much that I almost didn't even include it in this book at all. So please hear me when I say that this verse, in context, is absolutely true. It doesn't mean that everything is gravy. When I was face down on the pavement just one trigger-finger twitch away from being shot on the spot, life sucked. It was not good. Now, you could argue that it's because I wasn't following

---

[2] Romans 8:28, English Standard Version.

God. You might say that God wasn't there because I had not pursued Him.

But I would argue that God was more present in that moment than at almost any other point in my life. He took a crappy situation and began, in that moment, to bring about a future that I could have never dreamed.

He set me up.

It is my hope that as you get to know the set-up that is my life, you will begin to see how you, too, have been set up by God to be who you never dreamed you could be and to do things you never thought possible.

The pages that follow tell some of the story of my life, but more so than that, they tell of the One who can set a person up like none other.

God really does cause all things to work together for good.

Here is one stunning example.

CHAPTER ONE

Diagnosis of "Normal"

Police. Guns. Drugs. Snitches.

Add those things together and you are likely tempted to just skip over this chapter on my childhood. After all, all ex-cons have basically the same experience during their adolescent years, right? I'm sure you already have a vivid picture in your head of mine.

You're probably thinking that I had an abusive and absent father married in name only to a drug-addicted mother who could never seem to leave the man who abused her. My entire school career was marked by suspensions, doing drugs in alleyways, and sleeping around.

That is unfortunately the home life that many convicts faced. The prisons are full of these heartbreaking stories of abandonment, abuse, and neglect.

It was not, however, my life. Not even a little bit.

Now don't get me wrong, there was some messed-up stuff in my family. In fact, I would venture to say that very little of my experience you would consider "normal," whatever that means.

Normal

Webster's Dictionary defines "normal" as "a type, standard, or regular pattern."[3] I'm not one to argue with the dictionary, but what if "normal" were so much more than that?

Normal, you see, is a chronic condition. Similar to a medical diagnosis, the sickness called "normal" can wreak havoc on a life. Just like the cancer that would wreck my childhood, "normal" can turn the promise of a bright future into the plight of a downward spiral into deep, deep darkness.

Normal is a condition we all suffer from in one way or another. It is passed down from generations before us, convincing us that we are destined for the same diagnosis that plagued our parents, grandparents, and great-grandparents. It persuasively convinces us that we are incapable of changing. Incapable of breaking out of the mold that we have been formed in. Unable, despite our best efforts, to be anything different than what we have always experienced as "normal."

> *Our "normal" past has an incredibly high chance of becoming our "normal" future.*

Psychologists say that our entire lives are influenced by what happens to us before the age of twelve. Another way of putting it is that our "normal" past has an incredibly high

---

[3] Miriam-Webster Dictionary, "normal", https://www.merriam-webster.com/dictionary/normal.

chance of becoming our "normal" future. This certainly has been a battle for me.

"Normal" is a condition that we all suffer from. A condition that, unless we are able to break free, plagues us forever.

Here is a rundown of my diagnosis.

Daddy's Normal

My grandfather was an alcoholic. He abused my dad and my grandmother until he passed away when my dad was just a kid. My grandmother quickly remarried a man, who as a step-father, was no different than my grandfather.

No, scratch that. He was different. Way different, in fact. He was so abusive that he made my grandfather look like a saint. In a letter I later found, my daddy wrote this about his step-father:

"I was raised up in total hell and never knew the true meaning of love or how to express it. My stepfather was the meanest man on earth."

As evidence that this was no exaggeration, when he was only fourteen, my dad ran away from home. Living an uncertain life on the streets would surely be better than living at home with that monster.

After running away at fourteen from the abuse and alcoholism that so wrecked his family, he stumbled upon a gig playing an extra in John Wayne's *The Alamo*. This stereotypical American beginning perfectly foreshadowed how he would influence me as my dad.

I am not certain what line of thinking led to this next development in his life, but Daddy ended up going back home. It is possible that the authorities might have sent him back after his brush with fame landed him in an orphanage, but just like in every boy, I can only think that there was a longing inside of him to be with family. The pastor at my church says that inside of everyone's heart are two chairs: one for mom and one for dad. Those two chairs can only be filled by those people. Others might try to sit in them, but it is impossible. They are either filled or vacant. Perhaps he thought he would make a last-ditch effort to fill the dad seat one final time.

Upon returning home, though, he quickly found out that nothing had changed.

Except, that is, for him.

As an adult, Daddy was about 6'0", 210 pounds. He was a big guy, which meant that by the time he returned home as a fifteen-year-old, he was a big kid. Gone was the scrawny punching bag from a year ago. This boy had hit manhood and could stand his ground, something he quickly proved.

After returning home, he wasted no time showing Sleepy (yes, that was really his step-father's name) that he was not to be messed with. Almost immediately, Sleepy tried to come at him, but instead of standing down, Daddy stood up. He grabbed Sleepy by the neck, threw him against the wall, and told him that he would kill him if he ever touched him again.

Knowing him, he meant every word of it.

At the age of sixteen, he left for good. This was probably a good move considering he likely would have served a life sentence for murder had he stayed.

Growing up too fast, Daddy was forced to figure out life on his own. He moved in with a friend in Houston and taught himself how to work on cars. Back then it was much easier because there were no fancy computers, just parts. He was smart, so it didn't take long before he taught himself how to work as a millwright, building and fixing heavy machinery.

A very short but significant part of his life was his military service. He actually only made it a couple of weeks. No, he was not dishonorably discharged for doing something stupid, that is unless you consider lying to get in to be stupid. When he was a kid, he shot out one of his eyes with a BB gun, resulting in having to have a glass eye. Somehow, he was able to fool

> *That's exactly what a set-up is: God taking anything and everything and using it for something greater than we can imagine.*

the doctor into thinking that his vision was perfect (how, I don't know–back then I can't imagine that a glass eye would be hard to spot), but the charade didn't last long. Not too long into boot camp, he was found out and discharged.

Why do I tell you this story? After all, it seems so insignificant, and indeed it was. That is until Daddy died, leaving my mom with three kids and no way to pay for a funeral. But because he was a veteran, he was able to have an all-expense paid funeral, lifting an incredibly heavy burden off of my momma's shoulders in the most painful season of her life.

This was the first time that I can remember really seeing God working things out for our good. That's exactly what a set-up is: God taking anything and everything and using it for something greater than we can imagine. He used a seemingly insignificant event in life as a way to make sure that our family would be taken care of during a time we didn't even know we would have to face.

It was one of the first set-ups I had ever experienced.

Mother's Normal

I love my mother.

Actually, as I've worked on this chapter, I've spoken to her more than a few times to make sure I have my facts straight.

Now don't get me wrong, this is not the reason that I love my mom, but I was (and still am) her favorite. Ask my brother and sister, and they will tell you the same thing.

She grew up in a very stereotypical southern home. Her mom, my nana, was as much of a southern belle as you're ever going to find, right down to the accent. Everything had to be proper, at least on the surface. That culture emphasizes the exterior much more than the interior. It was important for other people to see you at your best. To this day, my mom will not leave the house without giving herself a full make-over even though I have never thought that she needs it. She is so strikingly beautiful that I've always thought she looks like Farrah Fawcett.

Regardless of whether she needed it or not, growing up, she loved to look and feel pretty. The reality of it, however, was that what people saw on the outside was not always the whole picture.

I remember times when my mom would be so mad at my dad for staying out late at the bars every night or gambling their money away that she would throw plates and cups onto the ground, shattering them into a million pieces, all the while yelling, "I'll build a tent over this mess before I clean any of it up!" The stress of living with an alcoholic was real and affected her more than she probably knows to this day.

Even though her life was not quite as neatly put together as she looked on the outside, she was, and still is, a wonderful mom. She always gave us kids everything we needed and then some, and the tender way in which she cared for us after Daddy died saved us from even more heartache than we experienced.

Considering the hell we were about to go through as a family, at twelve years old, I needed a rock like my mother in my life. I thank God for her daily.

Labor Day, 1976 - A New Normal Begins

The date is one that I'll never forget. For many, Labor Day is joyous. It's a day to not work, to cookout, and to drink beer. For me, though, that day has lost its joy.

I had no idea how sick my dad was. I remember the headaches and the big, black mole on his back. I even knew that it was melanoma, a type of cancer that, as serious as it is today, was even worse back then.

For years of my childhood, Daddy was sick. Actually, it is hard for me to recall a memory of him when he was not battling the cancer. When I was seven, he went to a doctor in Houston for surgery. The surgeons thought they could remove the entire mole, curing him without any chemo or radiation. Sure enough, they performed the surgery, leaving a mean scar across his back, removing every trace of cancer from his body.

Or so they thought.

At this point, Daddy was on fire for Jesus. I don't mean that he went to church every Christmas. I mean the kind of Jesus freak who wears the cheesy gas station t-shirts. He loved Jesus and believed that Jesus had healed him.

Five years later though, he was still sick. I know in hindsight that this was a constant struggle for him, but to the twelve-year-old me, the whole thing was very sudden. My sister, brother, and I were at my aunt's home while Mom was at the hospital with Dad. I was outside playing, not really a care in the world at the time, when I saw Mom's cherry-red Buick LeSabre come rolling up with her friend behind the wheel.

My first inclination was to run to the car to see Daddy. *He's finally home!* I thought. The anticipation of hugging him, playing baseball again, and riding in the back of that truck some more is one thing I can still feel in my bones.

The feelings of excitement and relief that Daddy was finally home quickly faded as my mom, as serious as I had ever seen her, got out of the car. She brought us kids into the house and sat us down in the living room. My mind raced as I tried to figure out what was going on. "Did Daddy have to have another surgery? Is he going to have to stay in the hospital even longer?"

Instead, I could have never anticipated what actually came from her lips that Labor Day.

With quivering lips and tears flowing down her make-up covered cheeks she said, "Kids, your daddy went to be with Jesus."

The shock in my heart immediately sank in as if jumping into an ice bath after a long run in the middle of a Texas summer. Surely I had misunderstood. In a state of panic, I demanded that she tell me what was going on, still certain that there was no way that she meant what I had just heard.

"Danny," she said. "Your daddy died early this morning."

That's it. Seven words. Who knew that such a simple sentence could cause so much destruction in a matter of seconds?

"No! No! No! Not my daddy!" I wailed.

The pain was more intense than anything I had experienced in my life, and yet little did I know that it was just the beginning.

Some pain that life causes heals up nicely. A scar is left, but it was stitched up with care and precision and becomes barely noticeable. Other pain, however, heals, but it's ugly. It leaves not a one-inch scar but a big, ugly one like the scar on Daddy's back. That is what those seven words from my mother's mouth left in me.

I never got to say goodbye. Not that it would have eliminated the pain, but I can't help but to think that it would have eased the healing process. Had he been dying in the hospital, I could have visited him. I could have told him that I knew he was the best daddy he knew how to be. I could have let him know how much I appreciated the baseball games, truck rides, and times at the pool.

Instead, nothing. No final, "I love you." He was just gone. Just like that, Daddy was dead.

An Imperfect Superhero

Labor Day 1976 really did shatter to pieces what had been my normal life. After all, Daddy was my hero. I mean, isn't that true for most little boys? Sure, not every father lives up to the title, and some fail miserably, but inside of that little boy is something that says, *My daddy can do anything!*

"No way your daddy was perfect!" you might say. You'd be right. Absolutely right.

He had his vices. Actually, they were more like generational curses, those things passed down from father to son that just seem to automatically become a part of who you are. We all have them. Usually, they are our biggest battles in life.

Daddy's were drinking and gambling. Luckily for us kids, he wasn't a mean drunk like Sleepy but, boy, was he obnoxious.

9

I remember playing little league as a kid and hearing Dad badgering the umpires in his state of drunkenness. I still feel the shame that would overwhelm me as I just tried to have fun with my friends.

Aside from the drinking and gambling, I do have very fond memories of him, even at those baseball games. He was so invested in me. Granted, not in the way that other, sober dads were, but he cared.

I remember game after game when I would strike out (I was not the best baseball player, in large part because I was a scrawny little kid). It never failed that the end of the game was not the end of baseball for the day. We would go back to the field later that day, and he would throw me pitch after pitch until I would hit the ball. Looking back on it now, I can see with fondness how dedicated he was to me.

On other occasions, our time together had nothing to do with me getting better at something but, rather, were just fun. More times than I can count, I would ride in the back of his '63 Ford pick-up. For those of you who might be too young to remember, there was a time when it was legal to ride in the bed of a truck. I remember the feeling of wondering if I was going to fall out every time we would cross over the giant bridge heading out to Surfside Beach in Freeport where we would take mini vacations.

On another occasion, he used my suffering to get a good laugh. I mean, come on! What dad doesn't do this from time to time? I had always been somewhat of a picky eater, something that would end up serving me well later in life as a bodybuilder who could only eat the same handful of things every single day.

On this particular evening, our family was over at a friend's home eating a whole bunch of fish they had caught. I was a fan of fish sticks, but that was about it. Somehow Daddy convinced me to try a raw oyster.

"Just let it slide down your throat!" he said, making it sound so incredibly appetizing.

I did let it slide right down, that is until I immediately threw up all over the place. No sympathy from my parents that night. Just laughs at my expense. Luckily, I have been blessed with my own children now to whom I can pass on that experience.

This is how Daddy showed us he loved us. He was not very good with words. In fact, I'm not sure I ever remember hearing an "I love you." But I knew he did. He loved us by doing things with us; by investing his time in us.

Plain and simple, he loved us by being the best daddy he knew how to be. He didn't have anyone to show him the way, and he didn't have years to refine this whole dad thing. God gave him twelve years. That's it. And I will forever be grateful that he did with those years everything he knew to do.

The Man of the House

What were you doing when you were twelve?

I look at kids today and find it incredibly heartbreaking that they have to grow up so fast.

A twelve-year-old is a kid. A kid whose hormones are not even close to settled. A kid who still likes to play make-believe, ride bikes with friends, and tell stupid, gross jokes that only other twelve-year-olds find funny. They are not adults and should never have to be.

I was that the twelve-year-old kid on September 5, 1976, but the next day, September 6, I had to grow up. I was only one day older. A mere twenty-four-hours more mature. But, on that day, I became a twelve-year-old adult.

If I could count the number of times that someone put on my shoulders the title "man of the house" during that first year after Daddy died, I'd probably still be counting. I can hear the voices now:

"Grow up, son! You're the man of the house now!"

"Ain't nobody going to take care of your momma if you don't! You're the man of the house!"

The truth is that I never shied away from that title. I think deep down inside I believed it to be true. So, in the middle of adolescence, I took upon my shoulders the responsibility of being the man of the house, even though I was still a little boy. From that point forward, I was a good kid. Not wanting to let momma down, I followed all of the rules without exception. As we would go to church every Sunday, I took it upon myself to be the best Christian boy I could be so as to make life a little easier for Mom.

On the outside, I was indeed the man of the house. On the inside, though? On the inside, I was a broken kid. I had this gaping wound left inside of me from Daddy dying, and I was bleeding out.

On the inside, I was dying, but I was bound and determined to hold it together for Mom. I had to, because after all, if not me, who? Entering year thirteen and beyond, I had every intention of being the best "man of the house" that I could possibly be.

I mean, this was now my new normal, right?

Could it be that God had used the first twelve years of my life as a set-up? Was I set up, at the tender age of twelve, to become a man, never to touch the "normal" that had plagued Sleepy and my father?

CHAPTER TWO

Set in Motion

"O Death, where is thy sting?"
1 Corinthians 15:55

In my experience, death has a hell of a sting.

Coyote Peterson is a man who knows what it feels like to get stung. If you have never seen his YouTube videos, bookmark this page and take a break to go watch one. The guy is crazy. He travels the planet to find the world's most painful insects, proceeds to capture them, place them on his arm, and force them to sting him.

All you need to do is watch Coyote get stung by the bullet ant to understand the sting I felt when Daddy died.

Please don't hear me saying that the Bible is wrong when it questions the sting of death. In the light of eternity for those who follow Jesus, death has lost much of its sting. But here on earth, death sucks.

Death not only sucks, but it can completely change the trajectory of our lives. Every time we experience death, or any setback for that matter, it takes something out of us.

After Daddy died, I tried my best to put the anger on a shelf. After all, I really didn't think Mother could handle me being anything other than the picture perfect, rule-following, Christian boy.

> *Every time we experience death, or any setback for that matter, it takes something out of us.*

Even though I felt like I had been bloodied up by the first punch of round one, I hadn't been knocked out. I might have had a broken nose and swollen eyes from the punch of Daddy dying, but I was still standing.

How many times, though, does life just punch you once? I don't know about you, but these things never seem to be one-and-done.

A New Man

The first big punch in the gut after Daddy died was when mother decided to remarry. Don't misunderstand me when I tell you this story and think I fault my Mom for remarrying. I don't, and no one should if they have not been in her position before. But to a twelve-year-old kid who was still raw from losing his dad, having a new man in the house was difficult.

The situation wasn't made any easier by the fact that he was very abusive, both physically and emotionally. Honestly, it was the emotional abuse that took a toll on me the most.

When Daddy died, the only material item that he left us that was to be given to me was his nice set of Craftsman tools.

That's it. All of my memories of Daddy wrapped up in some socket wrenches.

Those meant the world to me, and my new stepdad knew it. That's exactly why he went in the garage, threw his tools in with Daddy's, and mixed them together. Because I had no way of knowing which ones were his and which were Daddy's, he kept them all.

It was vindictive to say the least.

Little by little, the new man in my house burned me out of everything I did before Daddy died. Baseball was no fun anymore now that there was no one around who cared two cents about what I was doing. It felt as if Daddy was dying all over again.

Tony

Tony was a friend of mine in eighth grade. He and I were not the absolute best of friends, but we were certainly close. One day that closeness took on a whole new meaning as during football practice he hit me harder than I had ever been hit before. I mean not able to walk, seeing stars kind of hit.

Many times after football, we would play a game of chess together. There are not many kids who will lay you out on the football field one second and play a quiet game of chess the next, but Tony would. We had a pretty cool friendship.

One day at school, we all thought Tony had suddenly gotten into the drug scene. He had never done drugs before, but this day we were positive. He was acting so weird like he had overdosed or something. When the paramedics arrived, even they thought he had overdosed, so they proceeded to treat him as such.

I wish it had just been an overdose.

Tony had come down with Reye's Syndrome.

Medical experts are still not certain what causes Reye's, but what we do know is that it can come on very suddenly and is very deadly. Those who do not succumb to death often live the rest of their lives with severe brain damage.

For Tony, all it took was about forty-eight hours before he died.

And just like that, the gaping wound that was left when Daddy died–the wound that by eighth grade was not healed but at least had a nasty looking scab over it—had been violently ripped open.

The bullet-ant sting of death got me again.

Tom

After Tony died in eighth grade, I managed to breeze through most of my freshman and sophomore years. Now that Daddy was gone, my love for sports had dwindled. The excitement of playing baseball with Daddy standing behind the backstop even more engaged in the game than I was had changed as Mom's new husband, my step-dad, couldn't have been less engaged in my life than he was.

I eventually made friends with non-sports minded boys my age. Tom and Tim were two of those friends.

We were close. Many times, we would be out on one of their family farms baling hay. It wasn't glamorous or even fun, but it (kind of) kept us out of trouble.

One afternoon, Tom and Tim were cleaning some guns in the kitchen at Tim's house.

Now maybe you grew up in the Northeast or somewhere else where you didn't even know someone who owned a gun.

Let me tell you, that was not the case in Texas. Tom and Tim, and just about everyone else I knew, had guns, and don't think for a second that they were careless with them. They were not. They knew what they were doing and were always very careful.

This one afternoon cleaning guns, though, a terrible accident happened.

I don't remember all of the details, but certain parts of the story I'll never forget. The two of them had been out dove hunting earlier that day. In Texas, it is more uncommon to *not* hunt than it is to hunt. When they got back to Tim's house, they did what any good hunter does after a day out. They assumed that the chamber was empty as they began to clean the guns that had just put away dozens of birds. Whether horseplay or simply a slip of a finger I'll never know, but when Tim's finger made contact with that trigger, Tom's life was over.

The truth of the matter is that this freak accident didn't only cause me to lose one friend, but two. Tim was still alive but, from then on, was just a shell of his former self. Riddled with guilt over what had happened, he withdrew from our circle of friends and never really came back around again.

There is something just plain wrong about going to a funeral full of nothing but tenth graders mourning the loss of their friend. Something that was always supposed to be reserved for those who lived long and finished well, I had only experienced in tragedy.

Daddy died too soon.

Tom died way too soon.

This was beginning to seem normal, and I didn't like it at all.

Jerry

Have you ever met someone who was so over-the-top when it came to joy that you just assumed that they were a fraud? You know, the kind of person who is always walking around whistling, singing, skipping.

Come on, man! Life can't be that good, you think.

Jerry Jackson was such a man.

Jerry taught my Sunday School growing up. Now I know you might have had some pretty crooked Sunday School teachers, those who would come and teach about how God hates liars, or better yet, those who droned on and on about loving others but would go home and treat their kids like crap.

Jerry, though, was different. To use the cliché, he practiced what he preached. He was not one of these hypocrites like most of the other Christians I knew at the time.

I remember the day vividly. Probably because this day, above any other since Daddy died, changed me.

That day I went to work at Covington's Meat Market, a place that was basically like a second home. At some point during my shift, the phone rang. When I picked it up, I heard my mom's voice. She would often call me at work to ask me to bring something home on my way back from work, but this time I knew something was different. In fact, I had not heard my Mom's voice sound this way since that day playing out in the front yard of my aunt's house when I was twelve.

"Danny," she said. "Jerry Jackson passed away."

I was completely numb, but this time, unlike when she had told me Daddy had died, I instantly believed her. Death had become normal.

Jerry died doing the one thing that defined him the most. That morning while he was driving, he noticed that a woman had broken down on the side of the road. In typical Jerry Jackson style, he pulled over to help her. Knowing him, there was never any question in his mind as to whether he was going to pull over.

The street was busy, and I think it might have been raining. Either way, the conditions were not the safest. As Jerry looked at the car and talked to the woman, it became apparent that he was not going to be able to fix it right then and there. The best thing was to first push the car out of harm's way into a parking lot. As he began to push the car into safety, he suffered a fatal heart attack.

Helping someone. Making this world a little better. Doing the thing so instantly that many men today would be unwilling to do. That was what Jerry Jackson was doing when he died.

The Turning Point

As if the first death of Daddy, were not enough, Tony, Tom, and especially Jerry, marked an abrupt shift in both my thinking and the way I was living.

Mother told me, every time someone would die, that it was just a part of life.

"People die, Danny. We have to keep on living."

I definitely knew that to be true. I knew that life did not stop when something tragic happened. Through all of the death, I kept working, kept going to school, and kept doing all of the other basic tasks that must be done to survive.

But the sting of death had numbed me in more ways than I realized. Experiencing so many people close to me die, I began to see death as normal. Of course, we all know that death *is* normal, but at least to Christians, it was never supposed to be.

Death *should* sting some.

Death *should* hit you right square between the eyes, leaving you a little bent out of shape. The moment that death ceases to affect you as a person is the moment that you know that you have become numb to the things that should startle you.

The problem for me, though, was not that I was numb to death; that in and of itself is really not that big of a deal. The thing that ended up making these crucial four years a turning point in my life was the fact that as I grew numb to death, I began to grow numb to everything else as well.

CHAPTER THREE

The Whirlwind

While much of my high school years were a blur, likely because I chose to forget everything, I do remember a defining moment at my grandma's house a few years before I graduated. This particular day did not seem like any big deal at the time, but looking back, I can see that it was another moment of being unknowingly set-up for my life to go in a direction I could have never dreamed.

As I sat in my grandma's living room, flipping through the pages of one of her many magazines, I came across an ad for *Muscle Magazine*. I remember seeing the men on the front page and thinking that I wanted to look like that.

If you've ever had a pipe dream, you know how I felt.

"Look at you, Danny. You're a scrawny little boy scared stiff because of your past. You ain't ever going to look like that."

The truth was, though, that I desperately wanted to look like those guys. I was certain that if only I could gain the level of muscle mass they had, I would be more confident, secure in my manhood, and, most importantly, would get all of the girls. I now know my fascination with looking like the guys in *Muscle Magazine* stemmed from my desperate desire to be a man. At the age of seventeen, even though I had been acting like a man, I still felt like a little boy. If I could look like that, I thought, then I would be a man.

Once I sent off the fifty cents to subscribe to the magazine, my obsession grew. I purchased my first cement weight set and started following every workout plan I read about in the magazine. Working out overtook every spare moment of my life. By the time senior year began, my efforts were paying off. As anticipated, I was more confident, secure in my manhood, and yes, the opposite sex actually began to notice me.

Throughout my senior year, my focus quickly shifted from the more honest understanding of what I had believed it meant to be a man to a lie the culture around me was screaming. Since Daddy died, I had my heart focused on living a morally upright, good life, not necessarily for me but for Mom. That is what I thought a man was, and to an extent, I was right. Daddy taught me that being a man meant stepping up to take care of those you cared about. It didn't mean not having faults, but rather working through your faults to be the person those around you needed you to be.

The place I found myself in by the time I graduated high school, though, was different. I was less focused on others, including Mom, and more focused on me. I had stopped thinking that if I wanted to grow as a man, I would need to keep going to church and caring for those whom I loved, and instead, I bought into the lie that manhood was about me, my happiness, and my looks.

This shift in thinking would end up being much more damaging to my future than I could have ever imagined.

Freedom

Upon graduating from high school in 1982, like every eighteen-year-old, I wanted nothing more than independence. While I did not move out of Mom's house for about six months, I did immediately get a "big boy" job at Houston Lighting and Power (HL&P) working at the Baytown service center. I worked as a lineman, and even though I was still working my way through training, the pay was much more than what I expected coming straight out of high school.

So far, so good.

While working at HL&P, I graduated from the cement weight set in my bedroom to an actual gym at Body Maintenance in Deer Park, Texas. It was while working out there that I met a few friends, one of whom owned the gym. Harold and Elizabeth were a couple who competed in both single and couples bodybuilding tournaments. They invited me to come watch a couple of them to see if it was something I might be interested in.

To them, I had what it took to compete. They looked at me and saw a good build, ideal symmetry, and a work ethic that would take me places. Although I still saw a scrawny, broken kid, I took a chance and began to work with them as I prepared to compete for the first time.

During this entire time, I was driven by the most intense hunger I had ever had for anything in my life. I was always, and I mean always, in the gym when I was supposed to be. I monitored every single calorie that went into my body, and I didn't allow my mind to focus on anything except for getting bigger. My routine was as spot-on as any other bodybuilder in the business, but the routine alone was not what took me to the next level.

During this time, the gym quickly became my place of worship. It made sense considering that my appearance had quickly become my god. Every day, I learned more and more about the science behind how to build muscle, a science that I still know the ins and outs of today. I feel confident that I could write another book solely about how to build muscle.

I was not only disciplined but incredibly passionate. Building muscle was my source of happiness, and that drove me to keep pressing on. Unfortunately, for all of the discipline and passion I had for building physical muscle, my desire to build spiritual muscle was not even on my radar.

As we began to really train hard, I started to believe in myself. The more rigorous my diet and workouts became, the more I liked what I saw in the mirror. Harold got me in contact with a photographer and choreographer to work on fine-tuning the skills needed to really excel, and before I knew it, I was standing on a stage, carefully flexing every muscle in my body for a panel of judges.

While on stage, I felt like Arnold Schwarzenegger, but when I looked at the pictures after, well let's just say that pictures don't lie. The good, the bad, and the ugly are on full display. No matter how badly you want to change things, you can't. We worked on a few minor details before competing in the 1985 A.A.U.S.E Texas competition. Much to my surprise, the hard work paid off, because I walked off that stage, in only my second-ever competition, a champion. I found my pictures on the inside of a few fitness magazines and realized that, in a very short time, I had become one of the men in the magazines that I had ordered just a few years ago.

On the outside, I was making it. It literally took only thirty-six months to go from a boy wishing that I could look just a bit manlier to a bodybuilder gracing the inside of professional magazines.

That was on the outside. On the inside, though, I was a jerk; prideful and self-centered. The façade of getting bigger, looking better, and being more successful was only there to cover up the fact that after all of these years, I was still more broken than I could imagine.

The "Benefits" of Success

As is often the case, the more successful I became, the more fun I began to have. The short but endless cycle of working, partying, working out, and recovering had become an almost daily norm. At this point, the partying just consisted of heavy drinking. I figured that everything was under control because, unlike a lot of the guys I ran with, I wasn't into the hard stuff.

Yet.

Somehow in the middle of the drinking and partying, I found a way to keep competing. Between the years of 1982 and 1985, I competed in a number of different competitions, many of which I won, in addition to trying out swimwear modeling. As is often the case, though, the more success I had, the more I fell away from my routines. I went to the gym less, didn't care as much about what I was putting into my body, and surrounded myself less and less with people who would encourage me to succeed.

In 1986, as all of the success continued to go to my head, I realized that if I was going to catch up with the groups I was running with, I was going to have to up my game.

Not my lifting game; I was plenty ahead in that area.

I was going to have to step up my partying game.

It was that year that I began to experiment with recreational drugs. I use the word "experiment" because it is common vocabulary today, but really it's a cop out made to sound like I just tried it a couple of times. The truth of the matter is that it did not take many months at all to be using drugs in much the same way I had been drinking.

Soon after trying hard drugs for the first time I was hooked, but my first time experimenting with them was not the best. Don't ask how I got into this situation, but the first time I tried cocaine was in the back seat of my z28 Camaro with a top-less dancer. It seemed overrated, that is until I found out that it was "bad stuff." Once I got my hands on the "good stuff," I was sold.

And, as if the slide down into the depths of immorality had not been steep enough, things were about to get even more out of control.

"Entertainment"

A couple of the guys I was working out with were in the adult entertainment industry. Now, let me stop here for a second. I know what you're thinking. To clear things up, I'm not talking about *that* kind of adult entertainment. I was vain, but even I had not gotten to that point yet. You might, however, think that what I did get involved in was arguably more humiliating than where your mind originally went.

The famous male dancing show Chippendales was visiting Houston for a long stint. My friends convinced me that I could make an enormous amount of money dancing. At first, I didn't think that I could stoop that low. There was something in my mind that was tricking me into thinking that I still had some dignity left. It didn't take long, however, to give into the allure of the dollar sign. After all, this could be a great opportunity to finally quit the power company job and focus full-time on body building and modeling.

The interview for this specific job was, shall I say, different. I will just leave it at the fact that for no other job interview in my life was I required to take my shirt off. While I did not have the dancing skills it took to be one of the stage dancers, my physique got me hired as a table host. Perhaps even more degrading than dancing on the stage, my entire job was to wait on tables of drunk women (and the occasional man) while wearing nothing more than spandex, a cummerbund, and a bow tie.

It took hardly any time at all before I realized that this was my ticket out of blue-collar life and into one focused on me. My new career path really was, in hindsight, a perfect picture of how I was living my life; focused on me and little else.

Luckily, I did not have to wait tables at shows long before I began getting invitations to perform. My first gig dancing on the big stage was with a group called Elite Male. The pure rush that came from dancing in these shows was unreal. I remember one show in particular in Arkansas. The week before we performed, the arena was nearly sold out for one of Country Music's biggest names. That weekend, though, when we pulled up in our limo, more people packed that arena to see us than to see the superstar the week before. I felt like a rock star.

By 1987, I was dancing full time, working on bodybuilding when I could, but mostly focused on having as good of a time as I possibly could with virtually no consideration of the toll it would soon take on my body and my life.

The deeper I got into the drug scene, the dumber I became in making life choices. As if my life was spinning out on control enough as it was, I had the brilliant idea of getting married to a girl who was also a dancer and druggie. As you could probably predict, that marriage lasted a whole seven months.

I guess it was just not meant to be.

The life cycle of waking up, working out, dancing, getting wasted, recovering, and repeating was a hell of a lot of fun for a while. The cash in my pockets and drugs constantly being pumped into my body gave me the continuous flow of adrenaline that I needed in order to avoid the fact that my life was spinning out of control.

Eventually, though, in 1989, I had a moment of clarity. I do not know where it came from, but I realized that if something did not change quickly, I was going to end up in jail at best or dead at worst. I had not, however, gained all of my senses back. Following the same course as last time, I decided that the best way to get my life back on track was to, you guessed it, get married...in Vegas!

I have no idea where this line of thinking came from, but for some reason, I thought that getting married would make me more responsible, especially if that marriage was performed by a fake, drunk Elvis. It certainly gave me more responsibility but did not in the slightest make me more responsible.

There was definitely, in the midst of the chaos, hints of normal. That is, after all, what it is like to be in a whirlwind. There are moments, like in a hurricane, that you find yourself in the eye. A friend of mine has a relative who rode out Hurricane Harvey in Rockport, Texas. According to their recollection of that night, when the eye of the storm was directly over them, the winds completely stopped. You could hear birds chirping. It seemed as if the storm was over, when in actuality, the worst was yet to come.

I was managing World Gym in Clear Lake, Texas, all the while working harder than ever on honing my skills to be the absolute best at what I did. There were days when my life seemed as normal as anyone else walking the street.

Those moments, though, were rare.

The Fight

In 1989, after a night of binge drinking and doing lines of coke at Club 6400, I had a run-in with the police that would all of a sudden make anything else I had ever done seem like amateur hour.

As I said, we had been drinking, among other things, like the world was going to end the next morning. It was not unlike all of the other nights, honestly, but this night, my new wife and I got into quite the argument. One of the parts of my old self that I am the most ashamed of is how I treated others, but especially women whom I was in a relationship with. The argument began to get physical. Luckily for her, there were a few police officers working extra duty as security. It took all of them to pull me away. Whether it was the alcohol, pure rage, or both I'm not sure, but I went down swinging.

This fight was no ordinary bar fight. I was pissed, and everyone knew it.

Punch after punch, kick after kick, and claw after claw, I let those cops know just how strong I was. When they thought they finally had me down, I bit one of the officer's fingers as hard as I could.

I literally gave them every ounce of everything I had.

Finally, all three of them were able to pin me down, but it took so much force that the pressure of their knees on my neck caused me to pass out.

When I came to, I was hog-tied and being dragged by the officers to the police car certain that things were over. This was a very unfortunate way to wake up because being hog-tied sucks. My hands were handcuffed behind me, my feet zip-tied, and then my hands and feet tied together. All of my weight when I was being drug was on the steel handcuffs, digging into my wrists causing excruciating pain even to someone numb from all of the drugs.

It didn't take long, however, to realize that I was in trouble. I was publicly intoxicated (to say the least), had threatened my wife, and had viciously assaulted multiple police officers.

This was no speeding ticket.

Luckily for me, I had resources from all of the dancing, and I was able to retain the services of one of the best criminal defense attorneys in the area. What should have been a slam-dunk case for the prosecutor turned into a fiercely argued jury trial because of the quick-witted attorney that I hired.

As I sat in jail, pending the outcome of my jury trial, I was honestly remorseful. From this point forward, I was convinced that things were going to change. That very second, no matter what happened with the trial, things were going to be different. I had a resolve that I had not had before, and I was fed up. Fed up with the endless spiral that my life was on. Fed up with having nothing to live for except the next show or binge.

By the grace of God, my jury trial ended in a not guilty verdict. It must have been God's grace because I was definitely guilty. But I took this as my second chance, and this time I was not going to let anything screw it up.

Had this whole mess been a set-up also? A wake-up call from God to get my act together? The final warning shot?

I got clean, stopped drinking and partying, and focused almost exclusively on my next tournament. My attendance at my church (the gym) became routine again, and the little dancing I was still involved in was simply to help pay the bills while I worked hard. I fine-tuned my diet so much so that I knew every single calorie going into my body and the purpose that it was serving.

All of this hard work paid off when I competed in the biggest competition of my life, the Lee Labrada Classic. I stunned everyone, including myself, with my conditioning, symmetry, and posing routine. As I stood on that stage as not only the champion of my weight class but the overall champion, I couldn't help but to ask myself how in the world I was able to get there, all the way from that jail cell not one year prior.

Hard work. Determination. Strength.

I had all of those things, and it had paid off. At least this time.

CHAPTER FOUR

The Set-Back

D reams.
We all have them. From the little boy or girl who dreams of doing things that jaded adults know is next-to-impossible, to the grown man or woman actually living out the very dreams they had as kids, everyone's life is built around, at least in part, dreams.

I fell into the latter camp. I was literally living out the dreams that I had dreamt for my life not three years prior. The accomplishments to my name were longer than anyone expected this early on in my career, and with the very exact formula, I had for building muscle, there were no signs that things were going to slow down.

The dream was alive and well.

Up to this point, though, the success I had found was accomplished solely based on my own strength.

I thought I was bulletproof. I thought that the roller coaster of a life I had lived had taught me all sorts of valuable lessons that made me strong enough to withstand anything.

What I didn't know was that life has an annoying way of testing your strength just when you get to the place where you think you're strong enough for anything. It is in the moment when you think you are strong enough that life always seems to throw a curve ball that makes your once rock solid strength buckle underneath of you.

The Miracle Pill

My own strength was not everything it was cracked up to be after all.

The first major set-back in my adult life occurred after my "top of the world" season. I had won the biggest tournament I had ever competed in, was as clean and sober as I had been in a long time, married, and finally thought that I had turned that page in my life for good.

Up to this point, I had been lucky that I had not experienced any major injuries or illnesses as a result of the constant heavy lifting. I had actually begun to think that I was invincible. Certainly a large part of this was due to my consistent working out, attention to detail, and caution against doing anything too dangerous.

But there was another ingredient in my ability to not just avoid injury but to also recover exponentially faster than most.

Not long into my career, I realized that my own strength alone was not going to cut it. The other guys, the ones who could lift twice as much as me for twice as long, had something I didn't have.

My coaches pretty quickly got me on a regular regimen of Anadrol-50.

Anadrol-50 is one of the most popular and effective oral steroids that has ever been on the market. It substantially increases red blood-cell production which, among other things, aids in ability and recovery.

I had quickly become dependent on this drug to do what I needed to do to get ahead. Again, there was no way I was going to compete with these other guys based only on my own strength. I needed some outside help and the Anadrol gave me that help.

This was good stuff.

The Set-Back

I remember the day vividly.

I was on a pull-down machine in the gym, a regular routine of mine for years. During one of the reps, I felt something pop. I had pulled muscles before, and, for a second, I thought I just tweaked something.

On I went.

A couple more reps in, however, it was apparent that I didn't pull something. The pain was so excruciating that I had to stop my workout mid-way, something I had never, ever done before.

Still thinking I had pulled a muscle, I got home and laid down. I figured that if I could just rest for an hour or so I would be good enough to get back and finish up my workout for the day.

Just when I had thought I was getting better, Christine, my wife at the time, jumped on the bed.

Nope! I was definitely not better!

You have to understand that I had an incredibly high pain threshold, so when I was in that much pain, something had to be wrong. Christine drove me to the hospital where, after a quick ultrasound and blood work showing a white cell count of over 18,000, I went into emergency surgery to repair a ruptured appendix.

The surgery went well, and I fully expected the recovery to go well also. After all, I could "help" the doctors speed up my recovery with my magic pill, Anadrol, something that would also help me not lose size from not eating enough food. I needed that medicine so much that Christine, as soon as I was out of surgery and awake, brought some to me. I figured that it was okay considering it would help get me out of the hospital faster.

Wow, did I have a way of justifying everything I was doing to myself.

I was not going to be bedridden a single second longer than absolutely necessary. I had been doing well in almost every aspect of my life. There was no way that was going to stop here. I would be back into the gym daily, training for the next national qualifier that came around.

At first my recovery went well, even better than the doctors thought it would (go figure!). After I was released, I began to have some minor problems with the drain tube that they had installed, but I was able to get back to work and into the gym on some level.

The real set-back came when I realized things were not going back to normal as quickly as I had assumed that they would. Even the extra help from the Anadrol was not enough to get me back into top form, at least not as quickly as I wanted.

I kept working out, but not with as much passion and drive.
I kept working at the gym, but not as often.

I let the disappointment regarding my lack of progress derail me in the things that I was passionate about. Instead of spending all of my time at the gym, I traded in some of it for time back at the clubs.

I guess I decided that between Daddy dying, living with an abusive stepfather, being arrested, then divorced and now dealing with a failing body, I owed myself a break.

Instead of carefully calculating every calorie that I ate, I began to drink again, caring less and less about my long-term goals.

The slide was gradual, but eventually, what seemed to be a minor set-back became the one event that would literally wipe out all of the progress I had made in my career, bodybuilding, and in getting clean.

What is the most ironic part of the whole thing? The event that set me back so much was one of the only bad things that had happened to me since moving out of Mom's house that *wasn't* my fault, and yet, it's the thing that got me.

My dream, the dream that I thought I had firmly in my grasp, was basically dead. I had been given opportunities to revive it, to reshape it, or even overhaul it, but I didn't. Instead, this seemingly insignificant moment in my life led to a series of crazy choices that would make the bar fight, steroids, and drug binges look amateur.

My dream dying was the final ingredient in what would soon culminate in the worst years of my entire life.

I only wish I had known then what I know now to be the easiest way imaginable to avoid facing an unnecessary set-back.

CHAPTER FIVE

Crazy Choices

hoices. Life is full of them. The average adult makes over 35,000 conscious choices each day. Sometimes the choices we make are of no consequence. When we eat a meal or where we go to fill up with gas have very little impact on our long-term future. Other choices, however, are not that way. These choices have the ability to snowball.

Have you ever thought about the fact that every single one of us, you included, are only one or two bad choices away from ruining our lives forever? One or two bad choices, no matter how many good ones we have made in our past, can wreck not only us but those around us. The best, most straight-laced church boy can spend the rest of his life in prison on death row because of one or two bad choices.

It doesn't take 35,000 in a row.

Just one or two.

Here are a few of my, shall I say, crazy choices.

Crazy Choice One: Baking a Cake

After having faced the first real set-back of my adult life, I was in pretty desperate need of money. I was still working at the gym and had begun to dance a bit more for the cash, but it wasn't enough. I needed more.

Not long after my recovery from the surgery I met two guys by the name of Anthony Byrd and Nick Thompson. Anthony I knew from working at the gym. He was about my age and was from a very well-off family in another suburb of Houston. As the two of us became closer friends, we started to party together and met Nick.

The best, most straight-laced church boy can spend the rest of his life in prison on death row because of one or two bad choices.

Nick was older than us and worked in the oil and gas industry. He made good money and lived the lifestyle that we wanted to live. Our time partying together consisted of late-night poker runs, parties on yachts, and cash being handed out like it was unlimited.

Nick and a couple of his friends had a facility in Houston that they mostly ran their crane repair business out of. Some of it was run down, but there was a room on the property that oddly resembled a laboratory.

Hands down, the biggest drug of choice at the time was ecstasy. We called it the love drug. It made you happy, helped you to love literally everyone, and gave you an out-of-this-world, euphoric feeling. Even looking back on it now I can say that it was a lot of fun.

We had noticed that this particular drug had gone down substantially in quality. This was probably due to the fact that the DEA was increasingly seeing it as a dangerous, high-level drug in the same category as cocaine and heroin. It's like no one remembered that just a decade before psychiatrists were pushing for the FDA to approve it as a prescription for use in helping patients open up about traumatic events in their past.

Whatever the reason, the business sense in all of us saw an opening.

If the quality of the drug was poor, but demand was still high, then we had an opportunity to make money.

We already had the lab, and Christine and I had a spare bedroom to lend to the cause. After all, how hard could making this stuff be?

We found a handbook online that gave step-by-step instructions on how to make the best ecstasy. Easy enough.

We bought all of the equipment we needed – extractors, burners, beakers, and test tubes. We rounded up all of the chemicals and set out to do something we thought would be just as easy as baking a cake.

We tried really hard to make the good stuff.

We even had become friends with a guy who was a chemist and in school to become a pharmacist. To this day, I would never share his name with anyone because he is genuinely a good guy, but he reluctantly helped us figure out just the perfect combinations and processes to make the best ecstasy that anyone in Houston had tried.

This became my life. I was obsessed with figuring out how to do this just right. And honestly, I didn't really see anything wrong with it. Call me jaded or just plain stupid, but I really did think that I was just trying to help people have a good time while also making some serious cash.

Not for a lack of effort at all, I quickly realized that I sucked at this job. In hindsight, manufacturing drugs in the spare bedroom of your apartment is actually a good thing to fail at, and I did.

To my credit, I wasn't the only one who had failed – my partners in this were just as bad.

Crazy choice one seemed like it was fizzling out. Was this an opportunity for me to chill out some and focus on my actual job? Maybe it was once again a time to start fresh, to turn over a new leaf.

Nah!

It was just an excuse to move on to crazy choice two.

Crazy Choice Two: Hi, Mom!

I mean, what were we going to do? We needed more money. I know, a normal person would probably go get, I don't know, a job. A real job.

Not us. I think you can see by now that there were not many things about my life by this point that would be considered normal.

We did the only thing we could think of to earn more cash.

Sell cocaine.

We began with a lot of fairly small deals, an eight-ball here and there. It was working, but we wanted more. That was when we met a guy who was native Colombian. He had deep ties with the Columbian drug gangs and was about to help us with the deal of a lifetime.

I wish I could go back in time and tell the twenty-something me that getting involved with a Columbian drug lord was a bad idea, but you'd also think that I wouldn't need to be told that.

Anthony and another buddy of ours, Brett, set up a deal that would eclipse any other we had ever done.

I joined the two of them for a dinner meeting at the Texas Tumbleweed. The clients were two club owners from San Antonio. They wanted to purchase five kilos of blow. Now, I'm not trying to get off the hook, but I was not one of the major players in the deal. Really, I was only there to intimidate the clients.

At that point, I could take a steel butter knife in my hands and break it in half. Not bend it back and forth until it broke, but snap it in half. I was the insurance, if you will, that no one was going to mess with Anthony or Brett.

This was a big deal that involved serious cash, cash that not just anyone carries around. Being that we were dealing with over $80,000.00 in product, we needed to know that they were serious and not undercovers or something. Knowing that we needed to see the goods, one of the guys slid across the table a newspaper folded up in the shape of a square. Inside was tens of thousands of dollars of cash, all the proof we needed that they were legit.

We confirmed with our Colombian contact that indeed the five kilos were available and arranged for the deal to go down at a Chili's restaurant off of Fountain View Drive in Houston. Before we met there the night of the exchange, another of our friends, Roman, offered up his apartment to close the deal instead. Knowing that it would be more private, we agreed to the change of location.

We all rode over to the apartment complex together where Roman and Diaz, one of the club owners, went up to the apartment while I sat down in the car with Stamper, the other club owner. The Colombian who was bringing the product ended up only bringing one kilo at a time, nervous to deal all five at once.

As Stamper and I sat in the car waiting for the product to be delivered, we just talked. It is amazing looking back how normal our conversation was. With an almost $100k drug deal going down just yards from us, we talked about our families, jobs, and past times.

While we were talking in the car, waiting for the product to arrive, I noticed something that struck me as a bit odd. While Stamper was on the phone with Diaz, there was a guy walking through the parking lot wearing a sport coat. This might not sound suspicious, but it was the middle of July in Texas. No one off the job wore a sport coat.

If I had been an experienced drug dealer, this would have sent off a huge red flag, but being that I was fairly naïve, I chalked it up to a poor clothing choice.

Not long after this the product arrived, the gate to the complex opened and closed as the biggest payday of my life was about to commence. As the Columbian walked up the stairs to the apartment, I couldn't help but notice that the kilo of blow, $50,000.00 worth, was being carried in a cereal box.

That's one expensive box of Cheerios!

Call it criminal maturity maybe, but the Colombian was much smarter than we were. Once he delivered the box, he instructed them to not open it or close the deal until he was gone. He wanted to be out in case the thing went sideways.

As he stepped into his car and approached the gate, the gate opened and then closed behind him.

As soon as the gate closed, Stamper asked me to get out of the car with him. I wondered if everything was OK, but things seemed good so far, so I stepped out.

"Get down! Get down! Get down!"

Guns were everywhere, each of which was pointed directly at my face. Each second went by as if it was a minute. All I could hear was my heart beating.

I hit the parking lot fast. After all, I was a nice drug dealer.

Stamper was a cop. Damn club owner was an undercover. He escorted me up the stairs where Diaz had all of the cash, $80,000.00, laid out on the coffee table along with the product. As if that wasn't bad enough, out of nowhere, cameras and lights appeared.

We were officially the subject of the newest episode of "City Under Siege."

All I could think of to say to the camera was hi to my mom. Seriously. I'm sure she was proud.

Through the help of a private investigator, I later found out that this whole thing was a set-up from the beginning. Our "buddy" Brett had apparently been busted about a month before all of this happened. We had no idea, and that was by design. He had struck a deal that he would be cut loose on the first bust if he would help them bust us.

This was my moment of fame. A few years prior, I had dreamed of being on television one day, I just thought it would have been in an interview after winning a major body building competition. Being one of the stars in a new reality segment as one of the duped drug dealers was obviously not on my radar. But wait, there is a bodybuilding element of this crazy story.

Back when I was up and coming in the field, I went to a nutritional seminar and met a bodybuilder by the name of Rick Hill. Since then he had become a cop and was a part of the task force that got us that July night. As I was being loaded into the back of a car, he whispered in my ear

"You're not representing bodybuilding very well."

No. No I wasn't.

And just like that a couple of single choices had just led to who knows how much time behind bars.

Two choices. That's it.

~~Crazy~~, No, Terrible Choice Three

There is much I regret about my past life. Certainly running a drug lab out of my bedroom and trying to deal five kilos of cocaine are on that list, but those things were mainly stupid. Sure, people could have gotten hurt, and I would never suggest that you quit your day job to do any of that, but looking back on it, we were just idiots. We had seen one too many movies that glamorized drugs and money. I regret all of it, but I don't lose sleep over it.

I do, however, lose sleep over this one.

The biggest regret of my life was using my strength to abuse.

When I was married to Christine, I was angry. One night in a fit of rage, I came at her so forcefully that I broke her collarbone. It was so bad that Brett, the snitch, had warned the police that I was extremely dangerous.

He was scared of me. Many people were.

As I sit here writing, I really struggled with whether or not to even include this about my past. I am so ashamed of it that I really don't want to write this at all, but I feel like I have to.

If you are reading this and your anger has caused you to become abusive, stop. Put this book down now and get help. No one will think you're a coward, and no one will judge you. In fact, seeking help to change your ways might just be the most heroic thing you will ever do.

CHAPTER SIX

Processing

Just an hour before, as I was sitting in the parking lot with Stamper, I thought that I was about to hit it big. This was hands down the biggest deal I had ever been a part of. Sure, my cut wouldn't be as big as Anthony's and Roman's, but it would still be a nice payday.

Instead, I was cuffed in the back of a car on my way to be processed at county.

And, all I could do on the way to processing was process.

Process what I had done and what was going to happen.

Process through the plan I was going to somehow come up with to get out of this one, because, for as long as I could remember, I was always able to get out of things.

Always.

But as we pulled into the county jail that I had seen the inside of more than once before, I knew that this was different. After all, I had been almost gunned down in a sting that I'm sure the cops behind it all had meticulously planned out in a room with a chalk board at the front like you'd see in movies. I might not have been a big deal to many, but a dozen different officers knew who I was and had allocated numerous resources to bring me down.

This was a big deal, and for the first time in my life, I knew it.

As we pulled into the jail, it was time for processing.

From the moment I stepped foot in county jail this time, I was reminded that the entire process is designed to make you feel as inhuman as possible. The holding cell is big, but not big enough for all of the people they cram into it. The perimeter of the cell is lined with stainless steel benches, all facing a single stainless-steel toilet in the middle of the room. Let me tell you, there is no logical reason to put a toilet in the middle of the room.

For the entire fourteen hours I was in there, I laid on the cold, dirty concrete floor because all of the benches were taken. Eventually, I got called into an interview room where they identified me and told me what I was being charged with.

"...possession of non-crack cocaine of over four hundred grams."

"...fifteen-to-life."

Finger prints, pictures, and waiting. Lots more waiting. It was in that moment that I began to do something that I hadn't done a lot of lately.

I prayed, but not really for real. Instead of repentance, I was trying to cut a deal with the God that I still believed in, at least somewhat.

You know what I mean, right? It's those times that you go to God and instruct Him that if He is real, He has to come through for you.

Like somehow it is up to Him to prove Himself to you.

If He could get me out of this mess, I would straighten up and serve Him. I thought I was giving Him the authority to take control over the situation, but looking back, I should have known better. I was never going to give control of my life to anything or anyone not named Danny Williford.

When I went before the judge with Anthony, we were both shocked. We knew we had screwed up (not the language we used at the time), but we were not expecting what we ended up hearing.

The possibility of fifteen years to life and a $300,000.00 bond.

Where in the world were we going to come up with that kind of money?

And fifteen years to life? It wasn't like we had murdered someone. We sold some coke. Nothing more, nothing less.

Nonetheless, there we were. Sitting behind bars until we could come up with at least $30,000.00, the 10% of the bond amount that we would have to post.

Right after the bond hearing, Anthony and I were separated. Anthony had an easier road than I did at first. His parents were very well connected and ended up pulling some strings with a retired judge who was a family friend. I, on the other hand, was not so lucky.

As usual though, a good friend of mine, Mike, pulled through, as he always did.

He hired a guy who ended up being one of the best defense attorneys in the area. He was a former district attorney for Harris County who had turned to criminal defense. He had a stellar reputation amongst prosecutors and judges and guided my case flawlessly.

He managed to get me in front of the judge again for a bond reduction hearing, at which point my bond was lowered to $60,000.00. While still a lot, $6,000.00 was much easier for Mike, Christine and I to pull together than $30,000.00.

While out on bond, the case dragged on forever. We would have a scheduled court date where the attorneys would end up behind closed doors with the judge. What they all talked about so much I don't know, but it always resulted in the court date being postponed. This happened again and again for almost two years. It was as if one moment I was going to be put away for fifteen, and the next moment all of the charges were going to be dropped.

> *Simple changes can lead to profound changes.*

The ebb and flow of my court case mirrored my life while I was out on bond. You could probably take a two-week slice of my life during those couple of years and see everything from altar boy to axe murderer.

Really, there were only a few things I needed to commit to once out on bond that would so easily turn my life around.

Simple changes can lead to profound changes.

Specifically, there were two things that I changed almost immediately. One habit to start, and one relationship to mend.

Finally, I seemed to be off to a good start.

CHAPTER SEVEN

Fixed-Up

I have to admit that this was one of the most difficult chapters of the book to write. Most every period of my life up to this point, and even after, was straight forward. Sure, it was messy, but I was either off the deep end or holding it together.

When I was let out on bail on the cocaine charge, though, my life was anything but simple. The back and forth between sinner and saint, husband and adulterer, recovering addict and addict truly made this the most complicated part of my story to tell.

Bear with me.

A Valiant Effort

I'm sure by now you see a pattern in my life. Like many of you, I have always had a tendency to get into trouble, followed up immediately by a commitment to change my ways, at least in a way that didn't keep me from having fun.

In a sense, the two years after being let out on bail were no different. I had been busted and thought that somehow it would be easy to turn things around. After all, why in God's name would I ever want to risk going back to that place again.

In another sense, though, this time was different.

In the past, my mistakes were not necessarily life-changing. The bar fight was, well, a bar fight. Many of you reading this book have probably been in one of those. Running a drug lab, while terrible, didn't bring about any punishment because I was never caught. The cocaine bust was the first time that I was really, truly in big trouble.

I thought that this time was different, because unlike the others, I knew that one more wrong move could result in life in prison.

When I got out, I immediately began to take steps to change my life. These things I did off and on the whole time my case was pending, not knowing how it was going to ultimately turn out. I wish I could say that I started down this path of change because I really wanted to be a different person, but honestly, I was just trying to look good to avoid prison time. When you look at it that way, none of it was actual change at all.

One of the most important things I did was try and reconcile things with Christine. I didn't do a great job at it (I was still as much of a jerk as before), but I knew that it would look good to the judge if I could go to court dates with my wife on one arm.

Let me tell you, looking good is a bad motivator for fixing a marriage.

Nonetheless, that is what motivated me.

Looks.

I had always been about looks. My mom cared deeply about what other people thought and taught me to do the same. If the outside could change, then the inside would follow suit. Being a bodybuilder didn't help. As I grew into that part of my life, my focus on image only intensified.

Having a wife certainly helped my image, but there was one other thing that would help even more.

My mom was going to a small Assemblies of God church outside of Houston. I knew that if I could say that I regularly attended church with my wife and mother that I would look *really* good. Honestly, I did want to be there. There was something that was appealing to me about church, something safe.

The problem that I had was the same problem so many others have today. I thought that doing the right things would result in my life being changed. Church was not a place for me to go to grow closer to God but more of a magic wand that I thought I could wave over my life to magically change it.

The truth is that just going to church never changed anyone. I now know that real change is not about what you do but who you know. I was trying to do the right things, but I didn't know the one person who could change everything for me: God.

For a while, though, I was convinced that I had turned over a new leaf. I was not "really" doing drugs and was only dancing enough to earn some extra cash. After attending church for a few weeks, I approached the pastor about sharing my testimony with the youth group. I had been through a lot and learned many lessons along the way. These kids could benefit from hearing my story, but more so than that I knew that I would benefit.

Luckily for the kids, the pastor never let me do this. What, after all, would I have said?

"OK kids, don't deal coke or run drug labs. It's bad. I used to do that stuff but got caught. You can, however, be a stripper, do drugs every now and then, and cheat on your wife. Just avoid the big stuff and you, too, can be just like me!"

Every parent's dream.

While continuously trying to get my life back in order so that I would look good to the judge, I was also fighting my case with my attorney. One of the things that he had me do was hire a private investigator to get to the bottom of what really happened leading up to the sting. Maybe, just maybe, he could uncover the fact that I had been illegally set-up or something else that would sink the case.

While that never happened, this was when I learned how the sting started in the first place. He figured out that my buddy Brett had actually set up the whole thing to try and get out of some trouble that he had been in previously. We had thought that Brett skipped town right after the bust, but the PI found him working as a caddy at a golf course in Clear Lake. It was in his interview with the PI that he shared about how I had broken Christine's collar bone and could snap a steel knife in half.

You never know what someone truly thinks about you until you can break a piece of steel like it's a toothpick and have the gall to hurt a woman.

While the PI did not uncover anything earth-shattering about my case, the outcome in the end was about as good as I could have hoped for. After all of the back and forth, I received five years deferred adjudication. Probation was all I got. That really was luck.

What about Anthony? Despite all of his connections and luck up to that point, he was sentenced to fifteen years.

Not Enough

In between each of my attempts at change and true trans-formation were failures. One after the other.

As you read this chapter it might seem as if my attempts at positive change were more numerous than my screw-ups and all of the times I contributed to my continued downfall.

They weren't. Not even close.

While I tried to keep it together with Christine, I was not exactly Mr. Perfect. This was in spite of her never giving up on me. She gave me numerous chances. In fact, as soon as I was let out on bail and moved into Mike's house, Christine would come visit regularly. Despite still being very hurt by my infidelity, she had not given up. Not only was she going to church with me, she was doing everything she could to salvage the relationship.

I should have taken the lifeline, but instead, I started going back to see Amanda, my most recent ex. I could juggle two girls at once without them knowing about it, right?

Right. Except I was not trying to juggle two. I was trying to juggle three.

While Christine was working, I would be with Amanda, and while Amanda was working I would be messing around with other girls. I still saw Amanda as just a dancer and assumed that she was doing the same thing behind my back. One night while Amanda was working, I was at a bar with some other girl I had picked up. At the time, Anthony and I were still hanging out some while his case was pending. Amanda got off of work and came to find me but couldn't. Luckily for her, Anthony ratted me out.

Amanda found me at that bar with the other girl and laid into me. It was over with her. It was over with Christine. And, to top it all off, it was over with this girl who at that time was still nameless to me.

There went that.

The whole church thing went about like my relationships did. I stuck it out and put on a good face for six whole weeks.

Six weeks. Was that really all I could muster up? Apparently so, because after those short weeks, I was back to selling drugs, albeit only enough to make the money I needed to buy drugs. I couldn't commit to anything, including my career as a drug dealer.

A vicious cycle it was.

Despite the fact that the good definitely did not outweigh the bad, maybe there was still enough good to put a small dent in the downward spiral that my life seemed to be on. It seemed like there was considering the lucky way my so-called fifteen to life ended up.

The Spiral Continues

My "pull yourself up by the bootstraps" method of change most obviously didn't work. It was not successful at turning my relationships with other people around, and it was most definitely not successful at turning my relationship with God around.

It was also wildly unsuccessful at turning my relationship with the law around.

In 1992, one year after the cocaine arrest, while still staring down the barrel of a possible fifteen-year-to-life prison sentence, I decided that it would be a good idea to go out and have some fun. For a normal person, a night of some fun is usually no problem, but not for me. A simple night out turned into a cocaine binge.

No risk there, right? Actually, I recognized the risk early on that evening, so using good old Danny-logic, I took multiple tequila shots to try and take the edge off. While that might not have seemed like a smart plan, to my credit, I did call a cab to come pick me up.

I don't remember much after getting in the cab because I was so messed up that I passed out in the back seat. I guess the cab driver tried to wake me up and couldn't so he called the police. When the police arrived, they apparently did a better job at trying to wake me up, because when I finally came to I was so agitated that I began fighting them. This time it wasn't assault, but I resisted enough to get arrested on a resisting arrest charge.

That night my new home was the Pasadena County Jail, the coldest and most miserable jail I had ever been in. With no blankets and only concrete walls and a stainless steel bed and toilet, I thought my luck had run out. That Williford luck that had followed me relentlessly over the past few years couldn't even handle this.

The fifteen-years-to-life had just been sealed by nothing less than a bad decision to go out drinking, followed by a good decision to call a cab, followed by a bad decision to resist arrest.

Bad. Good. Bad. The pattern of my life.

While in the Pasadena County Jail, I ran into a cop who I had seen before. Turns out he used to buy steroids from me. I capitalized on that relationship (and perhaps a bit of a passive-aggressive threat of blackmail) and asked him to talk to the arresting officers. After a quick conversation, the officers decided to dismiss the case and let me go.

Dismissed. Gone. As if it never happened. The luck was back!

After that, I went through a short time of going back to church, focusing on turning a corner. I don't need to go into the details about this because you know how it ends. The same as all the other times.

After getting deferred adjudication for the cocaine charge, the spiral continued. I know, I was monumentally stupid for not taking advantage of the olive branch that had just been extended to me. To be honest, I tried but couldn't. I was powerless to change and wouldn't figure out why until much later.

As I reflect back, I can't help but compare the feelings of, on the one hand not wanting to change and on the other wanting to change but not having the power to do so. The most gut-wrenching place that I have ever been in was honestly wanting my life to change but feeling absolutely powerless to do anything about it.

In 1993, while waiting tables at the Mason Jar Restaurant in Houston I stayed after hours one night with the managers taking shots. Chalk it up to arrogance or learning from past experience, I decided against calling a cab. I was fine. I was invincible. If my luck could get me out of fifteen to life, certainly it could get me home.

Wrong. When I got pulled over, the comedy began. I say comedy because the dash-cam video of me trying to walk the line was funny to watch. It was like I was trying to surf the line instead.

I think I got an "F" on that test.

As funny as that part of the video was, the sad state of my life was on full display as I began to talk to the officers, barely intelligible from the slurring, about my dad and how much I missed him.

I didn't realize until then that an event in my life at the age of twelve still haunted me. I had not gotten over it, and while I would never today blame all of my past missteps on my dad dying, I will say that it definitely affected me.

As I plead guilty, once again, and served my twenty-day sentence in the Harris County Jail, I figured my deferred adjudication would be revoked. How many chances could I be given?

This time, though, just like the last, I received yet another olive branch.

Too bad I still didn't have the power to take it.

Fountain View

As I tried to start my life over for the millionth time, I moved into a new apartment on Fountain View Drive in Houston. This move more than anything else gives more insight into why my life never did change.

If you remember, the cocaine deal was originally slated to go down at a Chili's on Fountain View Drive.

Here I was, trying to make a fresh start in the same old places. Part of me wanted to change, but another part of me was stubbornly stuck in the past and the way things had always been.

> *Here I was, trying to make a fresh start in the same old places. Part of me wanted to change, but another part of me was stubbornly stuck in the past and the way things had always been.*

How could I have possibly changed my life without changing the places I hung out, the people I hung out with, and the things I did?

I couldn't.

CHAPTER EIGHT

Rock Bottom
(Really, this time WAS actually rock bottom!)

Have you ever been somewhere that ended up looking different than you expected? Maybe it was a vacation spot that you planned on going to for months and months. You had seen pictures, watched videos, and read reviews online only to get there and realize that it did not look the way you expected it would.

I thought I knew what rock bottom looked like. I had, after all, just gone through a situation that most people would consider rock bottom. If being pinned down on the ground in a cocaine bust, looking down the barrel of a fifteen-to-life sentence was not rock bottom, I'm not sure what would be.

After being released back into the free world, I experienced rock bottom. The interesting thing is that it did not involve police, guns, or drug busts. It did not include tragedy or death. This season of rock bottom did not look like rock bottom at the time. It looked like fun.

That, my friend, is where the deception comes in.

Her name was Michelle. Shortly after being let out of County, my friend Brian introduced us. Michelle was friends with a bunch of trust fund babies, so she had the money to do the things I wanted to do but was too broke for, not to mention that she was more than willing to help satisfy my sexual desire a few hours after meeting her.

The most important thing about Michelle for this story, however, is that she was my match.

I don't mean that she was my match in a one-true-love kind of way. She was my match in that she made my decisions look prude.

I was a liar. She was more of a liar.

I was an addict. She was more of an addict.

I was a dancer. She was a much better dancer.

I was messed up but put together on the surface. She was just plain messed up.

She was already doing stuff in her late teens that I had waited until my late twenties to do.

I had truly met my match.

We had a really good time, but I have to admit that it was strange to not be "the bad one." In fact, not being "the bad one" fed my idea that my attempts to put things together on the surface were working. The worse she was, the better I seemed. I was playing the comparison game, a game that makes you feel good in the moment but can come back to bite.

I call my time with Michelle my personal three-year binge. There was not a lot we didn't do, and there were not many days we were not getting high. Because she ran with so many wealthy business men who used her for sex as well as a lot of trust fund babies, we had access to all of the good stuff. She convinced me that I was missing out by staying with G-rated stuff like coke, so I began to experiment with crack and shooting up cocaine.

The "fun" was non-stop. We literally woke up, went out to breakfast, drank mimosas and bloody Marys, got ready to go out, went out and got wasted, went home to recover, then woke up and repeated the process again.

Rinse and repeat.

I remember one season in which she got hired to dance at a high-end club in Mexico City. I was "fortunate" enough to be able to go with her. We were literally treated like VIPs; everything we needed was right in front of us. She was making at least $3,000.00 per night, and we were partying like we had never partied in the States.

This was our life, and at the time, we thought it was pretty great, but even in the midst of this I would try and get cleaned up from time to time. The problem was that unlike Christine, and even Amanda to an extent, Michelle had no interest in getting clean. None. She had not grown up in the church or even in a semi-normal household. Her dad had severely sexually abused her, and she had spent years basically being pimped out by rich business men looking to exploit her brokenness.

She had no interest in becoming whole because she didn't know what being whole even looked like, so instead of humoring my efforts to become clean, she simply had me convinced that it wasn't possible.

As depraved as the drug binges and sexual dysfunctions were, the part of this three years that made it rock bottom for me was the deceit. It was the complete demolition of the little bit of character I still had left that actually made this truly rock bottom.

Before this point, I had made some really terrible decisions, but I had remained a fairly honest person. There were things Mom had instilled in me that I had, at least in part, hung on to.

That integrity, though, was gone, a fact illustrated by more examples than I can count.

Over the course of time, Michelle and I began to fall from glory. Instead of penthouse suites in Mexico and trust fund babies, we were demoted to drug deals in Houston's notorious Fourth Ward.

One night, I was driving through that part of Houston to help Michelle with some drug deal. The Fourth Ward was undeniably the roughest part of Houston; thus, it was littered with cops just waiting to catch someone. I pulled up to a stop sign and proceeded to turn right, but failed to engage my blinker. Two seconds, later the lights from a cop around the corner were behind me.

I was busted.

I knew that I had to think of a solution fast or else my deferred adjudication would very quickly turn into fifteen to life.

Let me just say that having that threat hanging over my head was a terrible way to live.

Luckily for me, being a white boy with blue eyes helps you out with the cops in the Fourth Ward. I'm not saying that's right, but it is true. I knew that if they found out who I was, though, I would go to jail and my deferred adjudication would be revoked, so I thought fast and lied. I told the officer that I had forgotten my driver's license, but gave them my name and date of birth.

My name was David Williford, and I was born on September 19, 1972.

The cop had no idea that I was not my brother.

She bought the lie and gave me a ticket for failing to use a turn signal. Actually she gave my brother a ticket for failing to use a turn signal.

Not long after, I confessed to my brother what had happened. So he wouldn't end up going to jail for not addressing this, he had to go into the courthouse and get it all sorted out. It wasn't easy. He had to take his time card from work to prove that he was at work, not driving in the Fourth Ward that day. Nothing happened to him, but my lie could have cost him his freedom for a time.

Once all sorted out, he and his wife tied the knot. I was in County, an unfortunate fact for me considering I would have loved to be at the wedding. His wife, though, hated me and was elated that I was locked up.

I had become pretty good at making enemies.

The embarrassing part is that I didn't care.

That instance was just scratching the surface. On more occasions than I can count, I would steal money from a girl's purse when they weren't looking. When they would notice that it was gone, I would act surprised and sympathetic and help them look for it.

One way on the outside, another way on the inside.

The three years with Michelle truly represented rock bottom in my story. You're not going to read the next chapter and see things go deeper. This was it. One thing that I want to make clear, however, is that I am not blaming any of this on her. She was hands down the most broken person I have ever met in my life, but I am the one who allowed myself to lose control.

She ran with me to the bottom of my pit, but I made the decision to go.

CHAPTER NINE

The Set-Up

The more Michelle and I partied, the crazier things got, but nothing could compare with what would happen one particular night at a club we frequented. That night, we had been partying pretty hard, no different than most other days, but this night was made more complicated because we mixed things that should never, ever, be mixed.

For the record, alcohol, hard drugs, boyfriends, and ex-boyfriends do not mix well.

One of my problems when in a relationship had always been my jealousy. I will say that you would probably have your guard up when it came to other men if you dated girls in the dancing world. In that world, people sleep around. It's normal, so I always expected it.

This night Michelle's ex was working at the bar of the club where we were. I don't remember anything especially over the line happening between them, but my jealousy kicked in, causing me to confront the man who I saw as a threat. One thing led to another, and I was in, yet again, another bar fight.

After being thrown out of the club, I knew I needed to get in the car and get out of there before the cops showed up. As I got into the car and began to speed off, a security guard was chasing me down trying to stop me. In the chaos and confusion, I ended up hitting the security guard with the car. I knew then and there that if I stopped I was for sure going away. The only option in my mind was to keep going.

A hit and run. Genius.

Later I would find out that Michelle and her friend had snitched me out, but at the time, I thought I had gotten away. Michelle came back to the apartment where we were staying, and immediately we began to figure out how we could leave town since I knew that they would find me if we stayed.

If you walked into our apartment, you would think that we were still running with business men and trust fund babies. We had the best TVs, furnishings, and appliances you could get. Of course, we didn't buy them. We told ourselves that we rented them from Aaron's, but in actuality, we stole them from Aaron's because we never paid our bill. It was normal for Aaron's collectors to come by about every two weeks, banging on the door demanding payment. We were "never home."

We still didn't know where we were going to go, but knowing we had to go somewhere, we took all of the furniture back to Aaron's. It was the right thing to do.

After all, we were all about doing the right thing.

Before leaving, we went on one last epic three-day binge, probably because we were all about doing the right thing. As I lay passed out on the floor of my apartment, wearing my name-emblazoned blazer that I had been wearing for the past three days, there was yet again a banging on the front door. I didn't even bother to get up, figuring it was Aaron's coming to get the furniture that I had already returned.

But when the door was kicked in, it was not Aaron's, and they were not there to recover furniture. It was a special Sherriff's Department and FBI joint taskforce tasked with apprehending aggravated offenders.

Now I could add "aggravated offender" to my resumé.

They ran over to me, stood me up, and asked if I was Daniel Williford. It took all of my effort to not be a jerk and point out the name that was on the inside of the jacket I was wearing.

They had found me, and now there would be multiple charges stacked on top of one another. My freedom would be gone. No more olive branches, no more good ol' Danny luck.

Then, as an FBI agent pushed my head down to put me in the back of her car, she leaned in and said, "Danny, it's time to get this behind you."

To this day, I believe with all of my heart that God was talking to me through her. I knew she was right, but I was scared. Scared that this time would be just like the rest. Scared that I had gotten too good at changing the exterior while being masterful at keeping the inside the same. But while in the car over to County this last time, I felt different. Not in a spiritual sense at all, but physically.

I was exhausted.

I was sick of myself, sick of my behavior, sick of my double-minded deceitful ways, and sick of always trying to be five people in one body. I was finally at my end. Luckily, God begins when we are at our end.

All through processing, I was in a fog. I couldn't think straight and honestly I don't remember much. What I do remember, though, is being more honest and transparent with God than I had been in a long time. I told Him, very bluntly, that if He was real, He was going to have to show me. He was going to have to make Himself incredibly tangible, or there was no way I was ever going to be able to come back to Him.

I couldn't just believe or muster up a tiny bit more faith. I needed to see something. I needed to see Him. Like the last time in County, I prayed, but this time was different. Last time, my prayers were all about me getting out of this mess. This time I can honestly say I never once asked for God to get me out of prison. I wasn't praying for my freedom. Instead, I was praying that God would show Himself to me and actually change me.

The next number of weeks I slept. It sounds like an exaggeration, but it's not. I had never been nor have I since been as exhausted as I was then.

In County, a few times each day the guards will ask the inmates to come out of their cells for count. I use the word "ask" lightly because it wasn't a question. The real harshness, though, came if you failed to heed that call. There were many times when I first came in that I would sleep through count. A guard would come into my cell, screaming at me, and I would only then barely wake up.

The easy way to explain my utter exhaustion is that my escapades had caught up with me. So many days and nights of binging would do that to anyone. But this feeling was different. I was totally checked out, almost comatose.

Sometimes things need a re-start. The computer I'm writing on right now needed one earlier today. It just wasn't working right. I would write a paragraph, and it would freeze. I would save the document, then it would freeze again. I knew that if I needed this computer to become what I needed it to be, I was going to have to restart it.

These couple of weeks of feeling zombie-like was God restarting me. My life had gotten so off track for so long that nothing other than a divine restart was going to do anything at all.

Once again, I was in what seemed like a bad place. It could appear to an outsider that this moment was rock bottom. I had fun with Michelle, but now, I had been caught and might never get out of prison again. In actuality, though, this was the set-up I had needed for years. It was the failure to stop and render aid, the FBI raid, and the county jail that God would use to actually reboot my life.

What was foggy before was now becoming clear: God had set me up, forcing me into a place where I would finally have to come face-to-face with my utter need for Him. As you'll see, the road there would not be easy, but it needed to happen.

CHAPTER TEN

Tangible

Even though I had been put through what felt like the restart cycle of a computer, I still needed something more. I had fooled myself before.

Dad died, and I needed to step up and be the man of the house, but I failed.

I needed to find a good career because dancing was going to lead to bad places, but I failed.

I needed to get back to church and straighten out my marriage, but I failed.

More times than I can count, I had been in a place of feeling like I was going to be able to turn things around.

I wanted to change. I really did, but wanting something is not enough. In the gym, it's not enough to want to bench 350 pounds. A lot of guys want to do that. In order to actually do it, you need the power. I had the desire to change, but I didn't have the power.

I had been around the church and religion long enough to know intellectually that any of my efforts at true transformation were going to fail without a real, vibrant relationship with God, but I had been doubting Him for so long, really since the death of Dad, that I felt incapable of just running back to Him.

I really did need Him to make Himself tangible. I needed Him to prove to me that He really was real.

Very soon, God would snap me out of the fog that had dropped down over me to meet me right where I was, giving me exactly what He knew I needed.

Real. Tangible. Proof.

Matthew, Mark, Luke, and John

As I began to settle into County, I figured that I needed to find ways to occupy my time considering I had no idea how long I'd be in. One of the first things I did was find some things to read. Reading always took my mind off of the fact that in prison one second seems like ten. I found in the law library a Bible that had probably been sitting there for quite a while. I had read some of the Bible before, but this time, as I opened to the first few pages of the New Testament, I began to see things that I had not seen before. I would spend hours upon hours each day reading the Gospels while doing push-ups. I was still focused on building my physical muscle as I had been for so long, but for the first time in, well, ever, I realized that I needed to build my spiritual muscles even more.

Matthew, Mark, Luke, and John, each word became increasingly real each time I read it. I can still picture the pages of that Bible, wrinkled up from all of the dried sweat that had dripped from my forehead while sitting under me while I did pushups.

God had already begun to make Himself tangible through the Bible, but I still needed more.

The Encounter

I was in County from September 1996 through May 1997 before I ended up being transferred into the prison system in Amarillo, Texas. While there, I had an experience that changed my life because it was the first time that God really, truly, made Himself known to me in a tangible way.

Now, I need to preface this story with a disclaimer. There is a good chance you're either not going to believe me or think I'm crazy, and here's the deal; I don't blame you. In fact, if the tables were turned and someone else was telling me this story, it might take me a while to come to a place where I believed them. All that to say, I'm giving you permission to doubt my story a bit.

Nevertheless, this really happened, and for as long as I live, no one can ever take that away from me.

In County, each cell (at least on the medical floor where I was) had four people in four bunks. This one particular day two of my cell mates, one of whom was named Carlos, were in the common area doing what I could only figure to be some sort of witchcraft. In prison, you run into all kinds of people, and it seems that a lot of guys will cling on to anything that seems to offer a glimmer of hope, even if in the end it's empty.

Carlos was an incredibly friendly guy. He and I got close pretty quickly despite the fact that, as much as I thought his witchcraft stuff was weird, he thought my Bible push-up routine was even weirder.

I thought some strange stuff was going on, but I had learned to mind my own business and stick to myself, so I didn't think too much of it, that is until a couple of the other guys told me to come out where they were.

"Carlos is going crazy!"

Yes, he was. As I came out of my cell into what was supposed to be a pretty chill area to play games or watch TV, I could hear Carlos screaming, crouching on top of the table like he was channeling his inner wild animal.

Remember, I was on the medical floor, so I witnessed crazy from time to time, but this was different. I was about to head back to my cell when Carlos locked eyes with me so tight that I was almost physically unable to walk away. Instead of seeing me, though, it became evident that he saw someone else.

> *Jesus, the one who I read about during every push-up, lived in me. He wasn't contained to a book or some stories I had learned as a kid. He was in me, and at that fact, even the demons shudder.*

"Jesus! Jesus! Jesus!"

Carols screamed this over and over again while staring intently at me. It was frightening stuff. I looked behind me thinking that someone was messing with him or something, but it was just me. No one else was there.

"Carlos! Where's Jesus?" I asked. All he could do is keep screaming.

"Jesus! Jesus! Jesus!"

At that moment, I had a realization that changed me forever; it will change you forever when you realize that the same can be true for you, too.

Jesus, the one who I read about during every push-up, lived in me. He wasn't contained to a book or some stories I had learned as a kid. He was in me, and at that fact, even the demons shudder. Carlos had seen Jesus in me, and because he was far from God, it terrified him.

As Carlos slithered back to his cell (yes, he literally slithered on his belly back to his cell), I did the only thing I felt was appropriate at the time. I walked up to him, not knowing if he was going to try and kill me or what, put my hands on him, and prayed. I don't remember exactly what I prayed, but Carlos snapped out of whatever it was that was going on.

Carlos was pretty quickly transferred out of County, probably to some sort of psychiatric ward because he had acted so crazy.

I'm not sure what happened to him after all of this, but I am certain of what happened to me. I knew that Jesus, the living God, was living in me, and that other people noticed. Once I knew that God Himself didn't just know about me from a distance but lived inside of me, everything changed. All of a sudden, I realized I wasn't just some messed up convict but an instrument for God's use.

Plead True

My entire life up to this point had been based on lies. I was a master at lying and had proven to myself that my lies could get me out of terrible situations. I knew, though, that this had to be different. Lying would no longer be my way forward.

The truth would set me free. Finding out what the truth was, though, was the hard part.

Even though the cocaine charge seemed to be behind me, the possibility of having my deferred adjudication revoked continued to hang over my head. Keep in mind that, although I had begun to get serious about my relationship with God, I was still a master manipulator, always thinking of the next angle I could take to get myself out of trouble. I started spending a lot more time in the law library they had available to all of the inmates, reading case after case to try and figure out what I was going to do.

Had I acted out of insanity? Maybe if I plead not guilty because of insanity I would get off.

But I knew that wasn't true and probably would not hold water.

When I was close to giving up, I found a newspaper article in one of the papers that the guards were so gracious to give us every day. In this particular story, a kid had been in a vehicular accident, hit someone, and fled the scene. At the end of the article was a brief mention that the kid had been sentenced to the max.

This didn't sound good for me.

But it actually was the break I was needing.

He was sentenced to the maximum, not for assault with a deadly weapon but for failure to stop and render aid.

"Plead true, Danny." I swear that I heard God audibly say this to me.

No sooner than I could put the newspaper down I made contact with my court-appointed attorney. She tried really hard, but I'm sure due to her overburdened case load, she just didn't have much time to look at my case. When I asked her, though, if we could plead guilty to failure to stop and render aid, she agreed.

I knew that this is what happened. After all, regardless of how bad what I did was, I did not intentionally assault that security guard with that car. I was stupid, messed up, and tried to get away too quickly. I deserved to pay for that, but I didn't try and assault him. Now though, I could finally own what I did wrong while not paying for something that I didn't actually do.

After deciding what we were going to do, I went to appear before the judge to see if this was going to fly. If you've never been in County and then had to appear before a judge in a courtroom, then you are unaware of the secret world that exists behind the judge's chambers. In Houston anyway there were a number of holding cells in the areas behind the chambers. Connecting the cells and the courtrooms were a series of underground tunnels that offenders are ushered through as they await their fate. Think about the walk from the cells to the electric chair shown on the movie *The Green Mile*.

It's an incredibly eerie feeling.

The judge ended up agreeing with me and allowed me to plead true to the maximum sentence for failure to stop and render aid. I was sentenced to five years in the state penitentiary. It's strange to think about now, but this was actually a huge victory.

Five years was a long time, but something inside of me knew that I needed this time away to make sure that this new change within me was the real deal.

If God was indeed setting me up for my life to finally be changed, I needed to allow time for it to actually happen. God had made Himself tangible to me in so many ways in such a short time, but I still needed time for the change to stick. It would be time alone that would make this experience different than all of the others.

Washed in Water

Another pivotal moment in which God was gracious enough to reveal Himself to me was when I was in transit to my final vacation spot at the Texas penitentiary in Amarillo. At one of the transitional facilities, some Christians came in to teach a class. Knock Christians all you want, but when you're in prison, you quickly realize that everyone will flake out on you except the Christians. They always showed up, no matter what, and seemed to genuinely care.

During this specific teaching time, I got baptized. Granted, it was not in a beautiful baptismal at the First Baptist Church in front of my friends and family, but it was sweet nonetheless. As I went down into the water in that old bathtub on wheels, I was reminded yet again that the old Danny was gone.

Over and over again, God answered my prayer to make Himself real. The fear that this was yet again some false transformation was still there, but inch by inch, moment by moment, I was becoming more convinced that the biggest chapter in my life was coming to a close.

And all of that before even stepping foot in the place that I would serve my sentence.

CHAPTER ELEVEN

Transition

As I wrapped up my time in County, my life began a major transition. I was moving from being a man who knew how to play the part but was really screwed up on the inside into someone who was beginning to be transformed from the inside out. And for as major as that transition was, it was accompanied by another one, only this one was physically not spiritually.

With County being as relaxed as it was, I would have been alright staying there for my entire sentence. Unfortunately, I was not sentenced to five years in county jail but in the state penitentiary. My assignment was beautiful Amarillo, Texas. If you've ever been to Amarillo, you know that I'm being sarcastic. Amarillo was just as brown as Houston was green, and so flat that when the meteorologist says the visibility is ten miles, it means you can actually see ten miles into the distance. The only thing that hinders visibility are the dust storms, which would make you think that the Dust Bowl of the late fifties has hit again.

Amarillo was certainly not paradise, but you know the saying: It's not about the destination, but the journey.

The journey was more humiliating than the destination.

While in prison, you move around a lot. When it comes time to leave one unit and move to another, you're called to join "the chain." The phrase makes it sound pretty horrible, and let me tell you, it is. That final time when I went before the judge in Houston, I was informed that Amarillo would be my new home. Like a college football player on draft day, I knew where I would end up, and though I was not as excited as the new NFL player, I was relieved to have some certainty.

All inmates in the state prison system have to process in and out of the infamous Walls Unit in Huntsville. Home to one of the nation's most notorious death rows, the Walls Unit makes things real. All of a sudden, this screwed up boy was being processed under the same roof that sees the execution by lethal injection of the state's most dangerous criminals. The area we stayed was stereotypical hard-core prison. Think steel bars, *Shawshank Redemption* style.

Talk about a wake-up call.

We were not in Huntsville very long, but one of my most grueling memories is from my time there. I had to be temporarily transferred to the third tier of a medical unit because I was having problems with a wisdom tooth. Now, having wisdom teeth removed is no one's favorite thing, but having it done in prison is beyond awful. The dentist literally has you sit down in a chair, and they pull it. Minimal numbing, and absolutely no pain medications afterward. Not even Advil. I'm actually missing a few of my molars because of the wonderful dental care that the state provides. One time I bit into a piece of candy, and because of the poor diet that we were served, my teeth had gotten softer, and I chipped a filling. Instead of redoing the filling, they just pulled the tooth. This happened a number of times and is the reason that a lot of these guys are missing most of their teeth. When in doubt, pull it. That must be the motto of the prison dental offices.

After this first tooth-pulling in Huntsville, I went up to my cell to "rest." The problem was that it was July, and my cell was on the top floor. Because heat rises, it was unbearable. The only thing guys did to stay cool was sleep with sheets that they had drenched in water. Uncomfortable, yes, but at least I was cool while I dealt with the throbbing pain.

After about five months, it was time to leave Huntsville, so myself and fifty other inmates caught a ride to Amarillo by bus. Get Greyhound out of your mind, because this bus was nothing like that. All fifty of us sat around the perimeter of the bus, hands cuffed in front of us. The bus was arranged this way so that there was room in the middle for the toilet. The drive was about eight hours total and the middle of the bus, with no barriers at all, was the only place to relieve ourselves. Talk about humiliating.

The drive was so long that half way there, we stopped at a facility in Abilene. When we got there, we had to go through the entire processing procedure again, get assigned a cell, and sleep for a few hours before finishing up the trip the next morning. I remember seeing all of the cotton fields overnight, wondering if when we got to Amarillo our job would be to pick cotton all day every day. The administrators in the prison system keep everything such a secret from the inmates that you honestly have no idea what the next day will look like, so all I could do was wonder what I would be doing.

When we finally arrived in Amarillo, I again noticed the white fields, but this time it wasn't cotton that littered the ground, but snow. Lots of it. I started to think that perhaps the heat in Huntsville was not as bad as the freezing temperatures in Amarillo would be. What I didn't realize at the time was that I would have to not only deal with the freezing temperatures in the winter, but also the excruciating heat in the summer. The quick fantasy that I had escaped the heat melted away come May.

The prison in Amarillo was a maximum-security unit, a fact obvious as soon as it came into sight. Most prisons you pass by on the highway are low-to-medium security, so there is razor wire around the perimeter, but they still don't look too scary. This campus, not so much. The razor wire was stacked three levels high on top of the tall fencing.

No one was getting out of this place.

The remoteness of Amarillo also reminded me of a very stark reality of my life, a reality that had not been the case for very long. Way out there, so far from anything I ever considered to be home, I knew no one was going to come to visit. My fear that I would be so isolated from everyone I knew proved to be mostly true. One of the things you will hear people who are experts on the issue of rehabilitation say is that the key to changing your life is to disconnect from old friends and influences. I agree with this completely, so the break from people of my past in the end was not a bad thing, but at the time when my whole life was being turned upside down, losing the people who I loved was difficult.

The more time that went by, the more I began to settle into my new life in Amarillo. I always prayed that the days would go by faster, but most days crawled just like the one before. Although the prison itself was basically brand new when I got there, there was nothing glamorous about my stay. I made the most of it, but prison is prison, and prison sucks.

CHAPTER TWELVE

If God Can Use the Mexican Mafia

Twenty-one months.

That's how long I spent incarcerated in Amarillo before being released, although it felt much longer than that. It is important to know that most people never served their entire sentence. They still don't. Depending on how overpopulated the system is, inmates serve only a certain percentage of their time given. I guess that is a cheaper way of controlling overpopulation than building new facilities.

It was great that my sentence was cut short; those months that I was there were not what many would consider fun. Since many of you will (hopefully) never spend time locked up for an extended period of time, I thought I'd give you a quick glimpse into what my life was like for this seemingly endless amount of time.

Renewing my Mind

One of the things that I took advantage of was the monotonous, boring, and isolated life I lived while locked up. With little to do, guys can choose to do a few different things. It's easy to let the isolation get the best of you, turning you into more of a bitter person than when you went in. I certainly knew a lot of guys who chose this path.

I, however, decided that I was going to use the time to renew my mind. By that time, I knew my weaknesses. I knew that I was top of my class in lying, manipulating, and doing just about anything to make a buck. I also knew I was good at putting up a façade to fool everyone into thinking I was something that I was not.

The Bible talks at one point about taking every thought captive to Christ. All that means is that we are to direct our thoughts toward Him and nothing else. In prison, this is surprisingly easier to do than in the free world because there is less for your attention. Instead of occupying my time with gangs, I joined Bible studies. On the surface, it looked foolish for me not to join a gang. In prison there is power in numbers, and all of the gangs vying for your allegiance feels like pledge week on a college campus for fraternities. I thank God that I was never tempted to join ranks because many of those guys basically threw away their chance at transformation because of a desire to be a part of a club.

The Bible studies, though, kept my mind off of everything else that was going on. I think I mentioned that one of the things Christians have always been good at is visiting the prisons. The same people from the same Baptist church would come every week to lead a Bible study. This regular time each week not only strengthened me but it changed the lives of a number of other men as well.

Those Bible studies were also a link between my mom and me. Often after Bible study was over, I would write her a letter telling her about the things I was learning and what God was doing in my life. She came to visit me once, but even though I did not see her often, I knew she was cheering me on from home.

A New Career

One thing that always happens in prison is that you get a new career. It's not glamorous, and usually, you get no say in it at all, but there is something unusually satisfying about having a job in a place with no freedom and very little ability to make a difference. It was in my job in the kitchen commissary that I found a little bit of purpose, something that ignited a spark in me when it seemed that hope was lost.

> *Idle time is the enemy to someone who is trying to recover their thought life.*

This job might seem menial to you, but it gave me purpose. My primary responsibility was to unload food trucks that would arrive and then distribute the food to the kitchens to be cooked. I had forgotten how bad prison food was until recently, when I visited a local prison to do some ministry and ate with some of the inmates. It's really, really bad.

One of the things about my job that most people would have liked but drove me crazy was that there were hours upon hours of idle time. Idle time is the enemy to someone who is trying to recover their thought life. You see, the more time you spend sitting around with nothing to do, the more your mind wanders back to the places you swore you would never go again. I knew that my time needed to be filled with something, so I took it upon myself to mop the floors in the commissary area. I have always been a clean freak, so this came second nature to me. I would mop it so meticulously that the floors would be pearly white at the end of each shift. It wasn't much, but it gave me an accomplishment every day, something that I could look at and say, "Good job, Danny."

As my time incarcerated went by, I worked my way up from the kitchen commissary to the school where I worked as a teacher's aide. While I had made stupid decisions in life, I was fairly proficient at reading and writing, so this was a good fit. I didn't get to do any teaching, but running copies and doing other tasks assigned by the teacher was better than unloading trucks and mopping floors.

I still remember the students who would come in to learn. Men, some of whom were over the age of sixty, who had no idea how to read or write. This gave the teacher, who was hired from outside of the prison walls, a difficult job. I always admired the students, though, for using their time locked up to better themselves and try and gain skills that would give them a leg up when they got out.

Praying

As I walked through serving my time, I did my best to avoid as much drama as I possibly could. Drama is never good, but honestly, it can be deadly when you're locked up with a thousand violent offenders.

When you follow God, though, He doesn't always keep you away from the drama. Instead, He often uses you to enter into the drama in order to bring peace to it.

> *When you follow God, though, He doesn't always keep you away from the drama. Instead, He often uses you to enter into the drama in order to bring peace to it.*

A few cells over from me was a very frightening looking African-American man who was a part of the Crips gang. This particular day he, for one reason or another, ended up having a seizure in his cell. I knew that the safest thing for this white boy was to ignore the situation and keep to myself. I also knew by this point that God didn't always ask me to do the safe thing. It became apparent to me that I was supposed to go into the cell, lay my hands on him, and pray for him. I knew how this would look; a white boy unaffiliated with any gang walking up to a Crip, putting my hands on him.

This was the kind of stuff that got people killed.

Nonetheless, I did what I felt God had asked me to do. Not long after I started to pray, the seizures stopped.

At this point, it would not have been outside of the expected to have a bounty over my head. You don't mess with someone who is part of a gang and not be targeted by that gang, and although I had not done anything wrong, the very fact that I was in there with my hands on him was enough to warrant my execution.

Luckily for me, nothing ever came of the situation except for the fact that once again God made Himself tangible in my life.

He used me and He protected me, a pattern that I have seen replicated over and over again throughout my entire life.

My Friend, Clavo

Going to Bible study allowed me to not only know the Bible better but also to get to know some interesting people. Sometimes people would come to Bible study just to have something to do, not necessarily because they were seeking to be transformed. One of these guys, Clavo, quickly became a good friend of mine.

It didn't take me long to figure out that not only was Clavo a member of the dreaded Mexican Mafia, but he was a sergeant-at-arms with the Mexican Mafia. Now, I'm not saying that these guys are good. Obviously they do a lot of bad, but one thing that I learned from my relationship with Clavo is that underneath the hard exterior, a lot of these guys are pretty nice.

At least, Clavo was.

One day, not long after skirting the possible danger I faced from the Crips, I faced yet another challenge. My cell mate, a guy who I also had become friends with, got into an altercation with a member of another gang, the Aztecas. The names of these gangs don't matter that much because they were all the real deal. When I walked into my cell, I saw my cellmate being pinned up against the wall about to be bludgeoned by this Azteca. Like I said, I never went out looking for a fight, but I would always come to the aid of a friend. I was still strong, so it didn't take much for me to drag the offender off of my friend.

I knew, though, that my effort to save my friend could turn out to be deadly for me. When you messed with one gang member, you messed with the whole gang. When I threw that one person on to the floor, I threw the entire gang on to the floor.

These guys would retaliate because they quite literally had nothing to lose.

Now, back to Clavo.

Not more than a day after the altercation in my cell, Clavo told me that he knew there was a hit out on me. To be clear, this meant that there was a challenge out there to have me killed.

Typically, this was the type of situation where there were consequences for staying out of gang life. The loner had no one to stand with him or to help fight his battles.

Luckily, though, I had Clavo. I'm not sure what all he told them behind my back, but whatever he said worked because no one ever messed with me. I assume that means that they didn't want Clavo to mess with them.

How amazing that God used a sergeant-at-arms in the Mexican Mafia to keep me, a white boy from the suburbs, safe in prison. Yet for however amazing that was, the way God used me in Clavo's life was equally amazing.

Clavo was not a believer before we started going to Bible study together. Remember, he was one of those who just went to stuff like that to stay busy and get out of their cell. Over time, though, he came to know Jesus in a really cool way. Once Clavo was saved, he began to write profusely to his family about the Jesus that he had come to know.

God used those letters to save the souls of his entire family. The eternities of dozens forever changed because a drug dealer and Mexican Mafia member decided to follow Jesus.

God really can use anyone.

Eventually, I was moved to a different building in the unit so Clavo and I lost touch. They move people around a lot to try and keep strong, unhealthy bonds from forming. But even after moving from him, he continued to look out for me. I got word that he had talked to his guys in my new building and asked them to watch out for me.

The deck was stacked against me. More than once there were those who sought to kill me, but God used Clavo to keep me safe.

Always remember, "If God can use the Mexican Mafia..."

CHAPTER THIRTEEN

One Last Chain

While prison definitely served a purpose in my life, and I'm grateful for that purpose, I never forgot that the goal was to get out. For security reasons, they never tell you when you are going home. Just a few moments before the bus ticket hits the palm of your hand you realize your time is done. Before then you just have to assume that you're being transferred to another unit.

On December 10, 1998, my name got called.

That in and of itself was nothing to get excited over. Again, all it meant was that I was going to catch a chain somewhere else, probably to another unit to serve the rest of my time. Unfortunately for me, I knew that at the time inmates with offenses like mine were serving approximately 50% of their time due to overcrowding, but when I heard my name called to catch the next chain, I couldn't help but get my hopes up.

I felt like a little kid on Christmas morning. Walking down the stairs and to the Christmas tree, you are almost positive that the gift in the box is the one toy you have been asking and hoping for all year. The excitement wells up to the point that, if on the off chance you're wrong, and it's just the box of socks that Aunt Sally gets you every year, you're going to be more than angry.

My hopes were officially up in the air. I had worked on my relationship with the Lord and my character was in a place that it had not been since I was a kid, but if this was not a journey to freedom that I was about to take, my character might backslide substantially.

That early morning, once my name was called, began the long journey that had brought me to Amarillo in the first place. Passing by those cotton fields that had given me so much unnecessary anxiety I couldn't help but wonder at the next turn my life was about to take. It was possible that my next destination would not be freedom outside the walls of the Texas Department of Justice, but rather a prison substantially hotter, older, and more run down than Amarillo

"What if there is no 'Clavo?'"

"What if they don't have Bible studies to help keep me on track?"

All of these questions had temporarily zapped the excitement of possibly going home right out of me, but not for long.

"I will finally get to see Mom."

"I can go to church, and really mean it this time."

"God, I better get released."

After stopping in Abilene to spend the night, we were on to Huntsville one more time. It was there that I would either be sent to my next prison destination or sent home. As we got closer and closer to the time where I was to find out my next step, time slowed down more and more.

Once to Huntsville, everyone was told their fate. Those catching a chain to the next prison that they would be housed in were booked back through processing. Those who were going home were shown instead to a room with some clothes to choose from. The clothes were awful, but much better than a chain to another penitentiary.

Let me tell you, I've never been more excited to put on clown clothes in my life. Literally, they were like clown clothes. The puffy tan pants, oversized shirt, and brick-like boots could be seen from a mile away.

But it didn't matter. I was done!

It seemed like only a few hours from the time I arrived in Huntsville not knowing if I was going to be a free man and the moment my bus ticket was placed in my hand. That moment is what so many inmates dream of as being the beginning of their new, free life. Unfortunately for so many, it's just the beginning of the next chapter of falling back into the same old things that got them there in the first place.

The Texas Department of Criminal Justice (TDCJ) does not give inmates the choice as to where they are catching a bus. We don't get to choose to go back to a parent's town or somewhere else where a fresh start can begin. Instead, all inmates are sent back to the place where they were arrested originally.

Back to where it all started. The same scenery, the same people, the same places to score drugs. To say it's hard to avoid the trap of falling back almost immediately is a gross understatement.

Those in the underworld of drugs and sex also know how to capitalize on this weakness. As soon as I got off the bus in

Houston, right there in front of me was a fork in the road. In one direction was freedom. My friend Mike was there to pick me up and take me to Mom's house. The freedom that had been denied to me was right there, steps away.

Also steps away, however, was a lifetime of continued bondage. Lining the street were prostitutes and drug dealers, waiting to capitalize on the weak men fresh out of a place with no drugs or sex. To partake was to satisfy an immediate desire but to also give up immediate freedom.

While I decided to walk right past the temptation and get in Mike's car, sadly, so many do not make that decision at all.

Home

When I finally got home, the reality of my new life took a while to set in. There were things about being out that were really nice, but there were also things, simple things, that took some getting used to. One of the first things was how deafening the silence was. In prison, everything echoes. Twenty-four/seven there is the sound of hundreds of different noises echoing through the steel and concrete halls and cell blocks, ringing in your ears at all hours. At home, there was nothing.

That sounds like it would be nice, however, I had apparently gotten used to the noise. My first purchase after getting home was a CD player. I listened to worship music on a loop, mostly because I wanted to keep my mind on those types of things, but also because I needed the noise to sleep or to focus on anything.

Work

I knew that I needed to do something to earn money. Of course, the option still technically existed to go back to dancing, but, in all reality, if I was to stay on the straight and narrow that I had committed myself to, it was no option at all. I needed a normal job just like I had when I moved to Houston years before and worked at the power company.

I got a job building scaffolding at Safway, one of the nation's largest sellers of scaffolding. It was not fancy, but it paid some of the bills and kept me busy. Every morning I would wake up at 4:30 a.m., drive Mom's car to work, and come home in time for dinner.

In a lot of ways, working in the free world was not much different than working in prison. I did everything I could to stay busy, using every moment to continue to pray and seek God. I know it sounds like I'm being a bit arrogant when I say I prayed for hours each day. I don't mean it like that at all. I was still messed up, and I knew that I was one bad move away from throwing it all away and going right back to where I had left off.

I prayed so much, not because I thought I was all that, but because I knew I was weak. Going to Him all the time was my only option. Without Him, I knew that I might as well give up and go back to dancing and selling drugs in apartment parking lots.

With Him, though, I knew the future could be greater than the past.

CHAPTER FOURTEEN

The Good Stuff

Recidivism (Back to Bad Habits)

Most everyone has probably come to expect some pretty intense stories of relapse to be a major part of any good ex-con's story. In fact, according to the U.S. Department of Justice over 75% of prisoners end up getting rearrested after five years.

It's not easy to be free.

My first instance of relapse happened in the summer of 1999. While at the gym, I ran into an old friend from my body building competition days. I had steered clear of the topless bars since being released, basically only stepping foot in my mom's house, places I was building scaffolding, the gym, or a church.

For some reason, though, I let my guard down and took him up on his offer for a night out. Once at the topless bar, the drinks stirred up some problem between him and me. It was so stupid that I don't even remember what we were mad over, but he ended up punching me square in the jaw. As we drove home, the argument heated up again and we ended up fighting hard on the side of the road.

Then, like guys do, we got out our anger, got back in the car, and headed back home.

It's funny how we can so easily drop things.

Luckily for me, no cops showed up. The only set-back was that I stayed home from work for a few days to let my face heal some.

And that, my friend, was the last time I dared look back in the rearview mirror. Nothing else since could have sent me backwards. I simply won't let it happen.

Conference

Not long at all after my one and only time of backsliding, I went to a small Pentecostal prophetic ministry conference near Houston. If you are new to the things of God or are not from a Pentecostal background and have no idea what I'm talking about, that's ok. The important thing about what happened is who I was when I left.

One note before I continue: I know that for those who are not believers or who are believers but have not been a part of the charismatic movement, the story that I'm about to tell might seem strange or even not from God. As with the demon encounter in County, praying for the Crip in Amarillo, or any of the other off the wall stories from my life, this one is real. I'd like to challenge those of you who are believers but might dismiss these kinds of stories because they just don't make sense to consider who God is. Is it possible that if we think we understand everything about who God is and how He works that we don't truly understand God? If God really is God, then there are going to be things that He does that our finite minds simply cannot wrap around.

This is just one of those stories.

These types of conferences are always attended by people who are wanting to receive a prophetic word from God. All that means is that sometimes God speaks through someone else something about your life. It's important to be discerning and test everything that is said to you to make sure that it really is from God, but it's pretty neat to actually get a word. In fact, it can change your life.

That particular day, I was there with a girl that I had made a lousy attempt at dating. In fact, this was one of our first dates and would also end up being our last. As we walked in and sat down on the front row, I couldn't help but get a little antsy hoping that God had something for me that day. As the conference continued, I sat with anticipation, wondering if God was going to pass me up.

About half way into the event, a friend of mine who happened to be playing drums, called out to me saying that the Lord wanted me to go sit by a lady by the name of Carolyn. Carolyn was another prophet who was attending the conference, sitting across the room from me but also on the front row. I thought it was weird, I mean I thought most of what was going on was weird, but, having nothing to lose, I went.

As I started walking towards her I felt what can only be described as the power of God coming into my body. My limbs began to feel heavy, and each step became harder and harder to take. About half way to her, I fell down on the ground, unable to keep walking from the heaviness of God's presence.

Having grown up in the Pentecostal church, I had seen people get "slain in the Spirit" many times. I always just rolled my eyes, thinking that it was all for show. Now I know that the enemy of my soul was just trying to rob me by keeping me from fully experiencing the Holy Spirit in my life.

After a few seconds, two men came over and picked me up. As I went over to Carolyn and she began to pray for me, I once again felt the weight and intensity of the Spirit of God so strongly that I went back, about twenty feet, actually slamming into a wall. As that happened, the gentlemen speaking called out to me from the pulpit, "Son, son. Today you are delivered."

Please know that by this time, my soul was already saved. I was going to Heaven, and there was nothing anyone could do about that. But, for as certain as my soul was saved, my mind still was not. I had won the battle in part of me by accepting Jesus as my Savior, but the other part, the battle in the mind, I was still fighting like crazy.

That day though, God delivered me.

That day, through all of the "weird Pentecostal stuff," I was actually given the power. The power to not go backwards but also the power to walk further into my calling and purpose.

Girls

As you know by now, I was always about the girls. Most of my adult life had centered around women. I danced with them. I danced *for* them. I cheated on them, used them, and abused them.

I was in a place in my life where I thought I had become quite the catch. I mean, come on. I was no longer dancing, would never even think about hitting a woman, and had a steady job making $8.25 an hour building scaffolding.

I was basically every dad's dream for his daughter.

OK. Maybe I wasn't yet the catch I thought I was. But, I was evolving.

With the exception of one girl I tried to date quickly after my release, I hadn't exactly been the ladies' man that I saw myself as.

Before, my evenings were almost always spent with girls. Once out of prison, that changed with the exception of Tuesday nights. Every Tuesday night, I was surrounded by women, but this time it wasn't at a strip club but a prayer meeting.

Apparently these meetings were seen as being so boring that I was basically the only guy who ever went. Most nights it was me, Mom, and a few other ladies. I'm kind of making fun of it, but in all seriousness, it was that season that developed me into a man who loves to pray for other people. It has become one of my main life callings.

Certainly there were other things I could have been doing with my life, but I also knew enough about myself to know that if I didn't stay completely committed to my faith things had a good chance of going south quickly. To this day, I honestly believe that the best way to stay close to the Lord is by plugging in to a good, Bible-based church.

The prayer group was only one of the ways that I was plugged in to this little church on the outskirts of Houston. One of the things you realize pretty quickly after being released from prison is that if you're going to make it, you can't do it alone. The guys who try and stay clean alone almost always end up going back to where they came from. It almost never works.

On the other hand, I've known guys who definitely don't go it alone but end up walking with the same crew they were with before they got arrested. That doesn't go well, either.

Intentional relationships with the right people are essential, not just for ex-cons but for everyone.

One of the other places where I found a relationship was the singles' group at the church. I have to admit that the thought of going to a singles' group sounded like torture to me. I always thought that those groups were for all of the nerdy kids who couldn't get any girl (need I even mention that while I judged all of those guys who couldn't get a girl, here I was, Mr. Ex-con, unable to get a girl?).

Once I finally got over my judgment, I found myself at one of the singles' meetings. While there, I noticed a petite brown-haired girl. I didn't know her name at the time, but I did know that I wished I did. I was definitely interested, but I tried not to be too crazy by just staring. It was perhaps the first time that I had eyes for a girl without lustful intent. I had started with one end in mind up to this point in most every relationship, and that was that it would end up in the bedroom.

This time seemed different.

I got invited to a friend's house for lunch after church not long after I had seen this girl. This friend was a scrawny kid who had asked me to help him bulk up. I convinced myself that the reason I was going over there was to help him monitor his meal plan and make some tweaks to his routine, but, really, I was going because the petite girl with brown hair was going to be there.

It was at that party that I first got to really talk to Kim.

I have learned over the years that, especially for someone with a story like mine, there are two different types of people.

Some people, upon hearing about who I used to be, either walk away, judge, or remain fearful, always keeping their distance and never allowing for real friendship. Others, though, embrace me. They recognize that we all have a past in one way or another and admire the fact that I got my life turned around. They come close and befriend me not because of what I've done but because of who I am. Nothing about my past scares them away, and around them, I feel as if I have no history at all.

I realized almost instantly that Kim fell into the second category.

That began a really fun, albeit short, season of dating. It doesn't matter how old you are, when you fall newly in love, it feels like you're in third grade again, getting that note passed to you from across the room. Looking back on it now, that's a key in making marriage work. I've always tried to be the same way now with my wife as I was back then when the sparks were new.

In November of 1999, only a couple of months after we had met, I was in the kitchen eating my lunch which consisted of a plain baked potato and a can of chicken. I was working on a jobsite nearby, and on occasion, we would hang out until late at night, so instead of her driving back to her house, she would often stay in my Mom's spare bedroom.

I've always been a fidgeter, so it was not uncommon that I was playing with the twist tie from the bread bag while I ate. When she came into the kitchen, I put the twist tie on her ring finger and molded it into the shape of a diamond ring; an ugly diamond ring, but hey, it was a ring. With just a twist-tie, my mom's old car, and an incredible salary of $8.25 an hour, I asked Kim to marry me.

The engagement was longer than the amount of time we had known each other prior to getting engaged. Over the course of the next five months, we saved for the wedding since we were older and couldn't go to our parents for money. If I'm honest, she did most of the saving, partially because she's an accountant, but mostly because she made way more money than I did.

We also made the decision to save ourselves physically for marriage. I would have never dreamed of committing to a long-term relationship with a girl, much less marriage, without "test driving the car" first. It's just what people did. Kim and I, though, decided to trust God, a decision that proved to be more than worth it.

We set a wedding date of April fifteenth because it was a big day in both of our families. We each had a grandmother with a birthday on April fifteenth, and it was Tax Day. With Kim being an accountant, we figured that adding one more positive thing onto the day would go even further in balancing out the fact that it was Tax Day.

As an added bonus, I knew there was no way I could ever forget our anniversary.

In the first month of our marriage, God made it very clear that He had us in His hand. One of my primary worries going into this was how in the world I was going to support a family. By the time we got married, I was making $11.00 per hour with dreams of upgrading our car and buying a house. Unfortunately, I didn't make enough to even pay our rent. Sure, Kim made enough so that my income was just supplemental, but that didn't sit well with me. I'm not saying that women cannot be the primary breadwinners in a home. But I will say that inside of every man is a desire to provide for his family, and I felt like I was going to fail in that area.

It couldn't have been more than two weeks after we got married that my boss called me into his office with an opportunity for me to move from building scaffolding to managing the operations of the small branch in Houston. The job was not only good career-wise but came with a raise to $18.00 an hour.

As if that wasn't enough, God answered my prayers pretty quickly about a house. Like I said, we both had a desire to own our own home. I think all newly married couples have that dream. The only problem was being a convicted felon made it hard enough to rent an apartment much less sign the note for a mortgage. By God's provision, none of that was even needed. Kim's grandfather was aging and moved in with Kim's aunt. He had lived in the same house for a long time and wanted to keep it in the family, so before putting it on the market, he asked if we would want to buy it from him.

We got a great deal, kept a family home, and became homeowners despite the odds stacked against us.

As He had so many times in prison and out, God once again reminded me that as long as I was following Him, everything was going to be alright.

Growing in Leadership

At the same time that I was growing in my marriage and career, I got an opportunity to learn from one of the greatest minds in leadership, John Maxwell. My pastor invited me to a conference that John was holding at another church in the area. As I sat there and listened to this giant in the field, I was mesmerized. I guess I never realized that this type of resource existed. I had assumed that I would grow in business by just grinding it out and working hard. Certainly that was a big part of it, but this conference opened up to me an entirely new idea that I could grow as an actual leader.

Being in prison takes a hit on your confidence. I know it did on mine. The thought that I, Danny Williford, would ever be a leader was foreign, but that night, I realized that my potential was much greater than I had ever thought.

> *If Maxwell had taught me anything, it was that the fear of failure will keep you from being great.*

It was then that I caught the leadership bug.

I started reading and listening to everything I could get a hold of by John Maxwell. I am a firm believer in the saying that "your mind is what it eats." This principle also works when it comes to your physical body too, by the way, but I was committed to filling my mind with things that would grow me spiritually and professionally.

Every forty-five-minute drive to and from work was spent listening to a mentoring series that John had just started doing. Every day, I was learning simple yet effective principles that obviously and practically began to take my career and my family to the next level.

Ever since that conference, I have consumed myself with all things leadership.

It was what I learned through John Maxwell that led me to a place in my career where I could support our family when our first child, Trinity, was born so that Kim could stay home with her.

It was also through the connections I had built up that I grew enough in my self-confidence to make a very important move when the opportunity came about. New Braunfels, Texas was never a place I had thought of living. I had built up a pretty good book of business in Houston, and it seemed as if the sky was the limit. The thing I liked most about where I was, though, was that it was safe. The risk of failure was minimal.

If Maxwell had taught me anything, it was that the fear of failure will keep you from being great. For the first time in my life, I both trusted God and believed in myself enough to jump at the opportunity to move to an area with Safway that needed work but was an untapped field of potential.

It was a risk, but how do you come by great reward without taking great risk?

Once I moved to New Braunfels, our family settled in. By that time, both my daughter and my son, Micah, had been born, and our family of four was, somewhat surprisingly, thriving.

Who would have thought?

Continued Blessings

Since being in New Braunfels, the Lord's blessings have literally been too numerous to count.

I still work at Safway, having alternated between sales manager and branch manager. In my time with the company, I have had the chance to bid on and close jobs providing scaffolding to remodel the governor's mansion, the state capitol building, and the LBJ Presidential Library. Ironically, because of my felony record, I am unable to pass a background check to step foot on to those job sites, yet I managed the whole thing from start to finish.

In 2008, I found that I was experiencing some minor health set-backs. When I went to the doctor, I was instructed to begin working out again and eating healthier diet. Knowing a fair bit about how to do that, I started to seriously work out and diet.

What ended up happening is that I realized I still had it in me to compete, only this time the right way. It was such a joy to get to compete in three competitions, one of which I won and one in which I failed miserably, albeit with the most important people in my life in attendance, my loving kids and my supportive, dynamite wife.

If you've screwed up in your past and it's caused you to have to leave some things behind, don't give up. Once you are healed, God will oftentimes reward you by letting you do things once again that you found so much joy in, only this time, you will do them the right way.

It's a really cool feeling.

I've also continued to be a student of all things leadership. Honestly, besides my faith, it's what has helped me excel in business as much as I have. In 2017, I had the incredible honor of attending the John Maxwell Exchange program, a one-week intensive leadership training, where I was able to get to know John and some of his executive team personally. It was such an incredible experience that, when I was invited back in 2018, I could not pass up the chance. This time we met in California and as part of the week toured the Dream Center. As soon as I stepped foot in that place, I knew exactly for whom this book was written.

The Dream Center exists to give those who have had addiction problems or otherwise difficult pasts not just a second chance at life but a chance to actually thrive. As I talked to just a few of the people there, I quickly saw myself in each of them, and I can't wait for everyone there to hear a bit of my story and feel a little more hope that they too can not just survive, but thrive.

Dream Center, this one's for you.

As I sit at the computer finishing up this project, I am reminded of one of the biggest and most undeserved blessings of all. Over the past few months, I have had papers spread out all over my kitchen table, tirelessly working on finishing my writing. All the while, Kim, Trinity, and Micah come in and out, reminding me without a word, why I am such a blessed man.

Please know that I am not bragging. I really don't deserve any of this, but that's the amazing part. None of us deserve anything we have. All of it, every part, is a precious gift from God.

How am I so sure? Did you even read my story? I'm not deserving, but I am so incredibly grateful.

Through all of my failures, God never deserted me. Sure, he let me make some pretty major mistakes, but, honestly, I wouldn't have it any other way, because it was through my screw-ups that God gave me set-ups, and those set-ups all worked together to bring me to where I am today.

No, I wouldn't have had it any other way.

CHAPTER FIFTEEN

Building Muscle

I often think back to the time in my grandmother's home when the spark inside of me to build muscle became a fire. Sitting there, looking at what could be, was exciting, but also very intimidating and demoralizing because I was so far from being where I wanted. At first it seemed impossible, but the more I put one foot in front of the other, the closer I got.

With every decision to eat canned chicken and a baked potato instead of a double cheeseburger, I got closer.

With every decision to go to the gym instead of sit on the couch, I got closer.

And with every decision to choose friends who would push me, I got closer.

There was never one moment that moved me instantly from scrawny fourteen-year-old to Lee Labrada champion, but rather thousands of decisions along the way.

I feel quite the same way today as I did standing on that stage winning my first competition: "How in the world did I get here?"

How do I have such an amazing family, a successful career, and once in a lifetime opportunities?

How did I go from peeing into a toilet in front of fifty other guys on the way to prison to where I am today? The answer to that question is the whole reason I wrote this book. It also looks a whole lot like how I built so much muscle.

This time, though, I built spiritual muscle, something so much more important than the physical.

The Power Source

I often get asked by people, "How do you build the muscle needed to compete?"

Part of the answer is expected.

To build competition-level muscle, you have to go to the gym more than often and do the right things when you're there.

To build competition-level muscle, you have to have someone who will hold you accountable, spot for you.

To build competition-level muscle, you have to eat the absolutely perfect diet, watching every single macro.

Those things are absolutely essential. Without them, no one stands a chance at building muscle to the point of being ready to compete. The struggle of so many, though, is that they think that's all they have to do. They don't understand that just going to the gym doesn't give you competition-level muscle.

Just having a good workout partner to spot you doesn't give you competition-level muscle.

Just eating the perfect diet exactly the way Arnold Schwarzenegger said to do it doesn't give you competition-level muscle.

Those things are essential, but without one additional thing, none of those things will get you competition-ready.

To have competition-level muscle, you have to have been built for it. You have to have the genetics coupled with a burning desire that most people will never have. This is something you have no control over, but serves as the power source for everything you do. If you have the right power source, you stand a chance at success. If you don't have the right power source, if you were not built for it, you're never going to compete as a bodybuilder.

I worked out with a guy a number of years back who wanted to get big. I had him on a strict diet, I was committed to working out with him every time he came to the gym, and I required that he hit the gym more than he wanted. He did those things for quite a while, but, honestly, he remained the same tall, lanky, strong-enough man that he was when he started.

Don't get me wrong, he made a lot of progress, but he was and still is lightyears away from being competition-ready.

The problem was that no matter the effort, he wasn't built for body building. He didn't have the right power source.

If you have the right power source, the effort will pay off. If not, the effort might help a little bit, but the goal will never be achieved.

Growing spiritually as a Christian works in quite the same way. There are certain things we have to do to build our spiritual muscle.

We have to spend time at church, regularly.

We have to have people around us to encourage us, motivate us, and help us lift weights bigger than we can lift on our own.

We have to feed ourselves the right thing, that being God's Word.

Most of this chapter is going to talk about what it looks like to do each of these three things, but the problem for so many is the same problem I had for most of my young adult life. In and out of prison, I thought that all I needed to do was start going to church or reading my Bible and my life would change. As you now know, it didn't.

And here's the truth as plain as I can make it: Yours won't either.

Like bodybuilding, there is one power source that you need in your spiritual life, and that power source is the one thing that will allow the changes you make in your life, like going to church, reading your Bible, and being accountable with others, to turn you into someone that you have only dreamed of being.

The difference, though, between the power source in bodybuilding and the power source in your spiritual life is that, in your spiritual life, anyone can have it.

The power source you need is Jesus.

Making the decision that I didn't want to live another minute of my life without having a relationship with Jesus Christ changed my life. The cool thing about Jesus is that He radically changes everyone who chooses to have a relationship with Him, including you.

Part of what happens when Jesus changes your life as much as He did mine is that you literally can't help but tell people about Him because you want them to see the same things happen in their lives.

No matter who you are, where you come from, or what you've done, I desperately want you to experience the same Jesus who so drastically changed my life.

What will happen, you ask, if you make that decision? Things might not turn around right away. I'd be lying if I told you it was a magic pill. After I was baptized, I still served over a year in prison, but during that time, He was working in me a peace that surpassed anything I had ever known, and He was building in me a resolve to never go backwards again. He was doing in me everything that I had tried to do in myself, but failed.

He will do the same thing for you, if you will just trust Him.

This includes, by the way, those reading this who have grown up in church, doing all of the religious stuff your parents taught you, but never actually surrendering your life to Jesus. Remember, no number of good works or religious activities can save you. Only Jesus can do that.

You have to have the power source.

If you are ready to take this step in your life, I'm asking that you simply pray the following prayer, right where you are, loud enough for you to hear it. If you have someone else around you who is a Christian, go get them and tell them of the decision you have made. Ask them to pray with you:

Jesus, thank you for the opportunity to make You
Lord of my life.
I have tried to do life my way and have failed. I now realize
that, without You, I am nothing, but with You, I am whole.
I give my life to You today, Jesus.
Now I am a Christian, and I get to spend forever
with You in Heaven.

Now, help me to live the life You want me to live.
In Your name I pray, amen.

If you just prayed this prayer, you, my friend, are a Christian!
Life is not promised to always be easy, and there will be some
difficult roads ahead, but trust me when I say that He has in
store for you a future greater than your past and a destiny that
you never imagined would be possible.

Building Muscle, Step One: Go to the Gym

Seems too obvious to even mention, doesn't it? I mean,
how in the world is someone supposed to get competition-ready
muscle without going to a gym (or something like CrossFit)?
While it seems obvious, people try other ways all of the time.
The truth is, though, that you're not going to get the same
results at home with a bench, bar, and weights. A professional
gym is going to provide you with tools to not just address the
big stuff, but all of the little muscles that matter just as much.
There is only so much you can do in your own garage. If you
really want to get to the next level in bodybuilding, you have
to go to a gym where the resources are.

On top of that, going every now and then isn't enough.
No matter how built for body building you are, if you only go
to the gym twice a year, your progress is going to be almost
unnoticeable.

You have to go when you don't feel like it.

You have to go when you are tired of it.

And you have to go even when no one around you is going
that much.

Still sound obvious to you? Why is it, I wonder, that we know the importance of going to the gym regularly to build physical muscle but somehow we miss the importance of going to church to build spiritual muscle?

The first key to building your spiritual muscle is to go to church regularly. Schedule it like you would a doctor's appointment. Like the gym, going to church on Easter and Christmas is not going to move you forward. All that does is help ease some guilt a couple of times per year.

Why go to church? Isn't the church full of hypocrites? Yes. Yes, it is. We are all hypocrites in a sense because none of us are perfect, but we all have the same goal of being more like Jesus each day. The church gives you resources that you don't have available by listening to some preacher on YouTube. They can help get you counseling, give you a small group to be a part of, and provide a place to receive healing that will never happen in your house.

If you have recently prayed to become a Christian, your immediate next step needs to be to get into a Bible-based church.

Go when you don't feel like it.

Go when you're tired of it.

And go even when no one around you is going.

Building Muscle, Step Two: Don't Go at it Alone

One of the keys to getting stronger consistently is to always be lifting a little bit more than you could before. This means that you're always pushing yourself, lifting ten pounds more than your body is capable of. Psychologically, this is really hard, because your mind knows that you can't do it. On top of that, there is great risk in lifting more than you can.

If you don't know what I'm talking about, just wait until three hundred pounds falls on your chest.

How do you get over this hurdle?

A spotter.

Having a spotter is the only way to lift more than you are capable of. With a spotter, your fear goes away. If you fail, he will make sure that weight doesn't crush you. All of a sudden, just having someone standing with you makes you feel like maybe you can do it. In fact, all it takes is that one extra person to make you realize that you actually are capable.

Building that much muscle is hard, but without a spotter, it's impossible.

Building your spiritual muscle is also impossible without someone beside you. I'm sure you've experienced being up against something that seems impossible. Often times, we simply walk away because, no matter the reward on the other side, we simply do not see that it's possible.

Often times, these types of things are not possible by ourselves. Walking through tragedy, heartache, or any other difficult experience is nearly impossible without someone walking with you.

The key is to find someone who is further along than you. You don't want a spotter who can only lift half of what you can. If you are a new Christian, find someone who is a picture of the man or woman you want to be someday, and ask them to walk with you. Let them into your life. Let them see the mess. The more they know, the more they can push you to be the best that God has created you to be.

Building Muscle, Step Three: Eat Right

The third step is the hardest one for almost everyone. Let's be honest. Going to the gym is fun. It can give you a rush of adrenaline, and having a few close friends who can work out with you and spot for you is fun: much better than being alone.

Diet, though, is a word almost no one likes. The diet required for a bodybuilder, though, is stricter and more boring than any diet you have probably ever been on. The purpose of every calorie is to achieve results. There is no fun involved. In fact, the people who know me are most shocked not by my workout routine but by my incredibly strict diet (although I've grown more relaxed over the past number of years: what can I say, I love Blue Bell ice-cream!).

It's not always fun, but it is the most important thing out of the three, because the results you get out of your body have everything to do with what you put into it. This is not just true physically, but psychologically also. Isn't it true that when you are purposeful about healthy eating, your motivation to workout goes up? In the same way, when your diet consists of McDonalds and Chick-fil-A, all of a sudden, you're not so motivated.

What you eat matters.

As a Christian, our spiritual food is God's Word, the Bible. Some Christians will tell you that reading your Bible will always be exhilarating. They will say that every time you open it, God speaks directly to you, and it changes your life in drastic ways.

I want to be more real with you than that. Sometimes when I read my Bible, there is no life-changing word from God. Sometimes I don't even do it because I want to. It's a discipline that I have instilled into my life, meaning I do it every day, whether I'm feeling it or not.

But I will tell you that God's Word has changed me. It continues to change me. This is because the Bible is God's written Word to you and me. When you read it, He will tell you things. He will tell you things about you and things about Him. It will become your source for wisdom when you don't know what to do and reassurance when you doubt God's goodness. But in order to get any of that, you have to read it.

I would recommend that you start where I did on the floor of my cell.

Matthew, Mark, Luke, and John tell the same story about Jesus, just from different perspectives. Start with Mark because it is the shortest, and every time you read, begin with a simple prayer:

> "Lord, thank you for Your Word.
> Now, speak to me through it. Show me something
> I have never seen before."

Hold Your Head Up

As I've said already, this book is not about me. It's about God and what He can do in your life. My story is just an example of what God can do with a mess, but what I want you to know is that He does it all the time.

The last few pages of this book are blank. No, it wasn't a printing error. The pages are there for you to begin to write your story, the greatest story ever told. Are you at rock bottom right now? Don't let this moment define you, but begin to write the story of how God is going to change your life through whatever it is you're going through.

Don't be fooled. You've been set up. It's hard when you're in the middle of it, I know. But it's not the end of the story. It's just the beginning.

Use the last few pages of this book to dream. What have you always wanted for your life that seems impossible or out of reach? Write it down, for with God all things, including your dreams, are possible!

I want to leave you with a quote by motivational speaker Les Brown:

"If you ever do something you regret, hold your head up.
If you ever make a big mistake, hold your head up.
If life catches you off guard, hold your head up.
It's not over."[4]

If you feel like it's over, know right now that it's not. Tell yourself that right now, out loud: "It's. Not. Over."

When you've been set up, hold your head up, because the one thing I know is that the best is yet to come!

---

[4] Brown, Les. "What to do When you Feel Lost (Les Brown Motivation)," *YouTube, https://www.youtube.com/watch?v=otiiFhqglAk.*

Notes

119

_____
_____
_____
_____
_____
_____
_____
_____
_____
_____
_____
_____
_____
_____
_____
_____
_____
_____
_____
_____
_____
_____
_____
_____
_____
_____
_____

Notes

About the author

Danny Williford is a successful business man running two multi-million dollar locations, a John Maxwell certified leadership coach, and champion body-builder. Most importantly, though, he is an ex-con and former drug dealer who had a radical encounter with a loving Jesus who absolutely changed his life. Today Danny lives in New Braunfels, Texas with his wife, Kim and children, Trinity and Micah. Danny's heart is to see those who are furthest from God be radically changed by Him and to become the leaders of tomorrow.

Endorsements

"A story of surrender and the journey to get there; but more powerfully, a reminder that Jesus chose you and he is waiting for you to choose. Williford exhibits the discipline we need to build spiritual muscle."

-Warden David G. Justice,
Federal Bureau of Prisons, Retired.

"If you need proof of the grace and mercy of God, look no further than Danny Williford's life story. His story tells of a life that had all the bad breaks, all the wrong choices, and all the dark results, but is finally punctuated with "But God!"

I've been privileged to walk with Danny for many years now and can attest to his sincerity and genuine faith. Though his story could easily be considered a jailhouse conversion, his life and love for Jesus and His church attest to the reality of a good God and the His mercy promised is evident and real.

Get ready to enjoy a good read and be blessed by the testimony of a very good God!"

-Dennis J. Gallaher, Pastor and writer

CPSIA information can be obtained
at www.ICGtesting.com
Printed in the USA
LVHW081308041219
639403LV00016B/745/P

9 781545 676516